AS I LAY WEEPING

Where Sorrow and Suffering Meet Faith and Hope

LINDSAY HIGDON

WESTBOW
P R E S S®
A DIVISION OF THOMAS NELSON
& ZONDERVAN

WestBow Press books may be ordered through booksellers or by contacting:

WestBow Press
A Division of Thomas Nelson & Zondervan
1663 Liberty Drive
Bloomington, IN 47403
www.westbowpress.com
844-714-3454

ISBN: 979-8-3850-1338-8 (sc)
ISBN: 979-8-3850-1339-5 (e)

Library of Congress Control Number: 2023922706

Print information available on the last page.

WestBow Press rev. date: 01/02/2024

For Natalie, Noah, and their sister in heaven,
Every day I wish you were here.
I love you, miss you, and hope I have made you proud.
See you soon.

You will never know the fullness of Christ
until you know the emptiness of everything but Christ.

—Charles Spurgeon

CONTENTS

ACKNOWLEDGMENTS

First and foremost, I want to thank my husband, Jason. I truly could not have done this without you. You have worked tirelessly alongside me through this process—from reading early drafts, giving feedback and suggestions, taking care of our children so I could sneak away to write, cheering me on, praying for me, supporting me unconditionally, and loving me through the emotional roller coaster that this project has been. Thank you for your deep knowledge and unrelenting integrity to God's word, which came in incredibly handy time and time again over the course of writing this book. Thank you for your resolve to love and live for Jesus no matter what and for always encouraging me to do the same. I hope that all six of our children (those in heaven and those here with us on earth) know how blessed they are to have you as their dad. I am beyond grateful to share this life with you. Thank you and I love you!

I also have to thank my children here on earth—Natalyn Lori Grace, Mason Noah, and Caleb Thomas. Thank you for always putting a smile on my face after all the tears that were shed during the writing of this book. Thank you for letting me (as best you could) take the time needed to complete this work—by napping long! I hope that years from now when you are older, you will read this book and learn about the impact that Natalie, Noah, and your other sibling in heaven made on me and your dad. And most of all, I hope that you will learn about Jesus and strengthen your commitment to live for Him all the days of your life. Thank you for the physical representations of God's grace that you are to me each day. Your mommy loves you!

To my dear Nonna, Donna Schutz, thank you for all the hours spent listening to me talk about this book, encouraging me, praying for me, and your willingness to help me. You got a sneak-peek look at several of these chapters, and your editorial suggestions were so helpful and appreciated. Above all that though, thank you for challenging me at an early age to grow in my relationship with Jesus. Apart from your persistent and unashamed nudges for me to read my Bible and spend quiet time with Jesus as a teenager, I'm not sure if my relationship with Him would be what it is today. And if that were the case, I'm not sure if this book would have ever come to be. Thank you for living your life so boldly and passionately for Jesus as it has taught me to do the same. I am so incredibly grateful for you as my grandmother, friend, and spiritual mentor.

I want to thank my mom, Lori Tunmer, for her role in this book coming to fulfillment. Your support to Jason and me following our losses has been absolutely essential and monumental for us—from coming to our house almost every day, bringing meals or cooking for us, reading the book *Hinds' Feet on High Places* to us, listening to us, crying with us, and just simply being there for us. Your support following our greatest tragedies helped shape our grief process, and this book is truly a culmination of that grief process. Thank you for who you are—your kind, generous, and joyful spirit shines the love of Jesus everywhere you go.

I also want to give special thanks to the pastors at the Mission Church, particularly Pastor Linda Schrek. Jason and I are forever grateful for how you walked alongside us in the aftermath of our losses—from visiting us in the hospital, facilitating Natalie and Noah's memorial service, praying for us, checking in on us, encouraging us, and being available to help us process what we were going through. You all have become our family, and I am truly grateful for how your support demonstrated God's love and grace to us.

To the WestBow Press publishing team, thank you for all your hard work and assistance to me throughout this process! Thank you for being available, working with me, answering questions, getting things done, and making this whole project happen in a practical way. I am thankful to have had a group of professionals on my side who are dedicated to Christian publishing.

And a final thanks to my stepdad, Scott Tunmer—you saved the day during my last-minute grammar crisis. Thank you for teaching me all about grammar when I was younger and for continuing to teach me! It has certainly been instrumental throughout this writing process.

INTRODUCTION

Childhood Dreams

What do you want to be when you grow up? To a child, that question incites so many exciting thoughts of endless possibilities, hopeful ambitions, and bright tomorrows. It elicits the best-case thinking for life's outlook. It provokes the idea that whatever we decide we want to be we can become.

That idea may be somewhat true to an extent. If I think back to one of my very first "what I wanted to be," it was, amusingly, a dolphin trainer. But living in the Northeast made it pretty impractical to *actually* become a dolphin trainer. As you grow up a little bit too, your "what you want to be" typically grows in maturity along with you.

Eventually, this childhood dream evolved into the desire to become a marine biologist. This seemed like a much more sophisticated want for a maturing child and much more pragmatic. *But*—and this is a big but—I have always been terrified of sharks. So once I learned that marine biologists spent a lot of time out on the ocean on boats, marine biology was out.

And so on it went. I think probably for most people, these "what we want to be when we grow up" are simply transient ambitions of our childhoods that change along with us over the course of adolescence.

For me though, there has been one "what I want to be" that

has never wavered, changed, or fizzled out over time: the desire to be a mom.

I was one of those girls who dreamed about getting married and having babies. It was a nonnegotiable. It trumped any and every aspiration, hope, or goal for my life.

I wanted to be a mom.

It seemed like a reasonable and achievable goal; after all, there are many women who get pregnant quickly or without even trying and go on to have a litter of kids with hardly any effort or heartache.

That is not my story though.

Shattered Dreams

I met the man who would become my husband, Jason, during my junior year at Southeastern University—a small Christian school in central Florida. We quickly discovered that we enjoyed spending time together and shared some things in common: we were both middle children, loved Jesus and the outdoors, played college sports, and had a strong desire to get married and start a family.

Jason and I were engaged after five months of dating and married seven months later at the ages of twenty-four and twenty-two respectively. Our wedding took place two days after my college graduation, and following our honeymoon, we moved back to my hometown in the Northeast to begin our married life.

About one month after that, we were excited to start trying to add to our family of two. But as years passed by and I still wasn't getting pregnant, we realized that something must be wrong.

After seeing my gynecologist and a reproductive endocrinologist, we found out that we both had major fertility problems that made it highly unlikely for us to get pregnant naturally. We were shocked and devastated, but we believed that God had a plan. After a great deal of prayer and consideration, we felt God leading us to move forward with investigating fertility treatments, specifically in vitro fertilization (IVF).

We educated ourselves about the IVF process and learned that it is very stressful, physically demanding, emotionally exhausting, expensive, time-consuming, and kind of terrifying. Yet despite it all, we prayerfully decided it was the right time to take that step and start the process.

By God's grace and provision, I got pregnant on our first IVF cycle—with twins! We were absolutely elated, ecstatic, grateful, happy, hopeful ... I'm not sure how else I can emphasize our level of excitement and thankfulness for our two growing babies.

At my twenty-week ultrasound, we found out that we were having a girl and a boy, whom we named Natalie Jane and Noah Jay. We were preparing our hearts and our home for their arrival and for life with them. I look back at this time in our lives and remember it as a time of bliss. It was ignorant bliss honestly. I fully expected my pregnancy to progress normally, lead to the healthy births of Natalie and Noah, and for them to come home with us.

I wish with all my heart that they had.

June 16, 2017

When I started experiencing signs of preterm labor, I truly had no idea what was happening. I realize now that I waited far too long before going to the hospital. By the time I arrived at the hospital's labor-and-delivery triage, I was in active labor and the doctor said that I was fully dilated. I was shocked to learn that I was going to have a baby that day, maybe two.

It wasn't until the doctor explained that I wasn't far enough along yet for the babies to be viable that I began to comprehend the gravity of the situation. The doctors could not stop my labor. Baby A, Natalie, was going to be born. And she was too premature to survive. I'm pretty sure I went into shock shortly thereafter.

Within about an hour after arriving at the hospital, Natalie Jane was born already in the presence of Jesus. I got to hold her as soon as she was born, and she was perfect. There are no words to describe the extent of pain, heartbreak, and horror that I experienced as I held her in my arms.

That night I didn't sleep. I just held her. It was both the best and worst night of my life, one that I will never forget.

June 17, 2017

After about thirty-six hours with Natalie, it was time to say goodbye. As much as I didn't want to let her go, my attention needed to turn to Noah. Saying goodbye to her was one of the most traumatizing moments—again, words just don't do it justice.

As the nurses took her body, it felt like a part of me was ripped away, and I broke.

No one should have to say goodbye to their child. With everything in me, I wanted her back. But in that desperate state, I could feel Noah in my womb moving around reminding me that *he* was still here with me. I wasn't alone, yet.

Despite our hopes for Noah's life, my labor continued to progress. That evening, he was born at 7:01 p.m. Noah's delivery was very different from Natalie's. Noah was born alive, and I got to hold him as he attempted to breathe on his own. Within a few minutes, he peacefully passed from our presence into the presence of Jesus and his sister.

I spent the rest of the night with Noah in my arms, as I had done with Natalie the night before. I am thankful to have had that time with each of them, but the nights were the hardest. The trauma of what had happened seemed to hit the worst at nighttime, causing waves of grief, fear, and panic that provoked me to cry out and scream.

I was terrified. I was a mess. I was broken.

The next day, I had to say goodbye to Noah. It was without a doubt the hardest thing I've ever had to do. When I let go of Natalie's body, if nothing else, I still had Noah. But letting go of Noah's body meant that I had no babies left.

Just like that, they were gone—and my life fell to pieces. *I* fell to pieces.

Desperate for Hope

The days of their births and deaths changed my life forever and changed *me* forever. Figuring out how to live again after losing them has been one of the greatest challenges—how to keep living in spite of and in the midst of my pain, loss, grief, and longing for my children.

I found myself in a place where I was absolutely desperate for hope, help, and emotional and spiritual sustenance—and the only place that I found those things was in Jesus. He alone sustained me in the days, weeks, and months that followed.

During that time, I kept a prayer journal that documented my time alone with God. The scriptures and prayers in the pages ahead come straight from that prayer journal, and more details of my story and experience are intertwined in each chapter. This book is a raw and honest reflection of my walk with God over the course of that painful time. It is an outflow of my heart for God and His heart for you.

In the midst of my greatest heartbreak, God was with me, led me, taught me, showed me mercy and grace, and—maybe the most valuable to me at the time—gave me reason to hope. For these reasons, I believe that it is my responsibility now to share with you the hope of Jesus Christ in the midst of whatever tragedy you may be facing—to share with you what I learned from mine, and encourage you that if I got through it, so will you.

I pray that God will speak to you as you read. I pray that He will touch you, comfort you, and draw Himself close to you—that He will use this book to help you find hope and strengthen your faith.

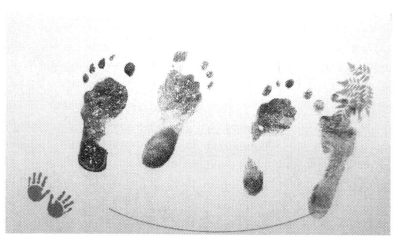

Natalie's footprints and Noah's footprints

When the Lord saw the grieving mother,
his heart broke for her.

—Luke 7:13 (TPT)

Dear Natalie and Noah,

This is your mommy speaking, and I can't believe that I'm writing this letter to you. I miss you both more than you can imagine and more than words can express. Without you, there are two enormous holes inside of me—and they will always be there. I need you to know how much I love you and that I would have done anything to keep you safe. I wanted more than anything to take care of you, be there for you, and spend life with you. You both have been the greatest joys of my life. I am grateful for the time I got to spend with each of you after your births, but it just wasn't long enough. I desperately want more time with you and wish I could be with you now. I don't know what to do now without you here. Our home feels empty, and I feel empty too. I am forever changed because of you, and I promise to carry you with me all the days of my life.

    In spite of my sorrow, grief, and anguish, I know that you both are OK and that you are safe. I know that you are being held in the arms of our Savior in the heavenly places and that you'll be waiting for me there. I believe that I will see you both again and that you will welcome me whenever that time comes. I hope that you will be happy to see me and that you'll tell me that you love me and have missed me too. I can't wait to spend eternity with the Lord and with you, and that is my hope, but it just feels too far away right now.

If I can be honest with you both, I'm struggling with feeling angry that you're gone and overwhelmed by confusion because I wanted so badly to be with you in this earthly life. But as I process what I'm feeling in the midst of this horror, in the midst of this terrible nightmare that I wish to wake up from, I know that I have a choice to make. I have a choice between being angry with God and turning away, or trusting Him even when it doesn't make sense. Natalie and Noah, I hope that you know your mommy enough even now to know that the former is not even an option, and it never will be.

I choose to trust my God, who is holding you both safely in His arms right now, even when everything in my life is falling apart and shattering around me. It's hard right now, and my flesh might not feel like trusting, but I'm telling you both that I've made my choice—that I know who my God is and that He is faithful and good. I don't know why He allowed you to die, but I know that He is the one who gave you life and knit you together within my womb. You were fearfully and wonderfully made by our Creator, and He has called you home.

Natalie and Noah, my heart is aching and broken as I long to be with you again. Please always remember that you are loved, wanted, and missed. I hope that God will read this letter to you—I'm not sure if it works that way, but there is just so much that I didn't get a chance to say even as I held you in my arms.

As I'm not sure how to walk in this life without you now, I realize that somehow someway I have to try, because I know that you would want me to. And I have to believe that my

Heavenly Father has plans to redeem and restore this in my life. Natalie and Noah, I will see you again soon after this earthly life has passed. And when I get there to heaven and embrace you in my arms, all my tears He will wipe away.

With all my love,
Your mommy

*The thought of my suffering and
homelessness is bitter beyond words.
I will never forget this awful time, as I grieve over my loss.
Yet I still dare to hope when I remember this:
The faithful love of the Lord never
ends! His mercies never cease.
Great is his faithfulness; his mercies begin afresh each morning.
I say to myself, "The Lord is my inheritance;
therefore, I will hope in him!"
The Lord is good to those who depend on
him, to those who search for him.*

—Lamentations 3:19–25 (NLT)

CHAPTER 1

As I Lay Weeping

Blessed are those whose strength is in you,
whose hearts are set on pilgrimage.
As they pass through the Valley of Baka,
they make it a place of springs;
the autumn rains also cover it with pools.

—Psalm 84:5–6 (NIV)

The days of Natalie and Noah's births and deaths are days that live in infamy in my life. The days that I spent lying in that hospital bed holding my babies who were already in the presence of Jesus are forever ingrained in my heart and mind. To take the words of the prophet Jeremiah in Lamentations 3:19 (NLT),

> The thought of my suffering and homelessness is bitter beyond words. I will never forget this awful time, as I grieve over my loss.

I will *never* forget that awful time, and I would never want to. The weeks that followed my loss mark a pivotal period in my walk with God as I was, for the first time in my life, in a place where my faith was really challenged. I was in so much pain, had so many questions, and felt so broken. I was on the verge of falling deep into the pit of hopelessness and despair, and I had to decide if I was going to let myself fall deeper or if I was going to try to climb out of it.

In my desperation immediately after their deaths, I searched for stories of other women who had lost babies. I longed to know that someone else had experienced it and managed to survive. I really wasn't sure how I was going to get through what I was facing. I didn't even know if I could, so I was desperate to find out if and how anyone else had.

Jason and I also looked up everything we could find about suffering in the context of God's sovereignty. We searched for Bible verses that spoke of God's comfort and grace. We found ourselves walking through our very own Valley of Weeping, and we needed to somehow find hope if we were going to make it through.

The psalmist writes in Psalm 84:5–6 (NIV),

> Blessed are those whose strength is in you,
> whose hearts are set on pilgrimage.
> As they pass through the Valley of Baka,
> they make it a place of springs;
> the autumn rains also cover it with pools.

The pilgrimage that the psalmist is thought to be referring to here is the journey that God's people were commanded to take back in that time period to worship God in Jerusalem. The Valley of Baka, or Valley of Weeping as referenced in other translations, is thought to have been a real place that worshippers of God had to travel through on their journey to Jerusalem. It is depicted as a perilous, arid place where there is no access to water. Despite the dangers and likely suffering associated with the passage through this valley, it was a necessary route for God's people to take on their way to Jerusalem.

I doubt that it is a coincidence that this valley is called the Valley of Weeping. Figuratively speaking, passage through this valley is seemingly unavoidable for us as God's people throughout the course of our lives. It is the valley that I was forced to walk through following my losses, and it may be the valley you are in now.

We read in Psalm 84 that as they (God's people) pass through this valley, they make it a place of springs. Another translation says that they make it a well. In other words, they find water in a place where there is no water to be found. And that is the same challenge that I faced and that you may now face except that it's not water we are searching for—it's hope. We need to find hope in a place where there is none, and the source of that hope is found through our personal relationships with Jesus.

In verse 5, the psalmist writes of those "whose hearts are set on pilgrimage" in reference to those whose hearts are set on God— obeying His commands, worshipping Him, and honoring Him. Our hearts too need to be set on Him even as we journey through our own grief, loss, and pain. Is it easy to do that? No, not really—pain can have the tendency to pull us off course if we let it. But the way through our valley is largely dependent upon our decision to remain walking with Him through it.

So while we don't need to literally pilgrimage toward Jerusalem, we do need to set our hearts on Him. And as we do, we may find wells in our valleys. In the midst of our very own Valley of Weeping, He will show Himself as the fountain of living water. As Jesus says in John 4:14 (NIV), "whoever drinks the water I give them will never thirst. Indeed, the water I give them will become in them a spring of water welling up to eternal life."

As we lie weeping in our valleys, He is the One who will lift our heads and point us to the wells. That is, He will be our hope in the midst of our suffering.

The valley may feel bleak, desolate, and hopeless, but hope *is* here and His name is Jesus. May His living water be poured over you abundantly today.

Journal entry from June 28, 2017

Lord, I need Your new mercies this morning and I cry to You. Father, I seek You here in this place of desperate heartbreak. Please forgive my frailness and my weakness as I struggle with fear and confusion over losing Natalie and Noah. I don't know what to do now, Lord, so I need You to show me. I look to You alone for I trust in Your faithfulness and Your promises. Lord, I believe that You are good to me. I believe that You are faithful and that You are for me. Lord, I ask humbly for a new vision from You, for a word from You. My hope is in You and I want to honor You with my life. I submitted and committed Natalie and Noah to You when they were in my womb, and Father, You are the One who gave them to me. And, Lord, You give and take away. I am choosing to trust You, Father, even though I don't know how I'm going to get through this or what's ahead. Amen.

I waited patiently for the Lord to help me,
and he turned to me and heard my cry.
He lifted me out of the pit of despair,
out of the mud and the mire.
He set my feet on solid ground
and steadied me as I walked along.
He has given me a new song to sing,
a hymn of praise to our God.
Many will see what he has done and be amazed.
They will put their trust in the Lord.

—Psalm 40:1–3 (NLT)

CHAPTER 2

THOUGH I WALK IN DARKNESS

I will lead blind Israel down a new path,
guiding them along an unfamiliar way.
I will brighten the darkness before them and
smooth out the road ahead of them.
Yes, I will indeed do these things; I will not forsake them.

—Isaiah 42:16 (NLT)

If you are walking in darkness, without a ray of light,
trust in the Lord and rely on your God.

—Isaiah 50:10 (NLT)

My losses left me in a state of complete darkness. I vividly remember the moment Jason and I left the hospital after having lost Natalie and Noah—there were no longer babies in my belly, and there were no longer babies in my arms. I remember sitting on the bench outside the hospital, holding the blankets that Natalie and Noah had been wrapped in as Jason went to get the car. Leaving the hospital without them was absolutely terrifying. It felt like all of a sudden I couldn't see anything in front of me. It wasn't that I couldn't see physically though; rather, I couldn't see what my life was supposed to look like anymore.

As we left to go home, I didn't know what home was supposed to look like without Natalie and Noah. I didn't know what tomorrow was supposed to look like without them. It felt as though I all of a sudden was living in a nightmare—so much so that sleeping felt like my only reprieve from the pain. While I slept, I didn't have to be consciously aware of my reality, but the problem with sleep is that you inevitably wake up. And each time I woke up, it felt like waking up to a nightmare, rather than waking up from one.

In this dark place, I couldn't see how I was possibly going to be able to get through it—I felt blinded by my pain. To quote Alain Bremond-Torrent, "There is not a lot you can see when there are tears in your eyes."

I also became ever so aware of how blinded I and we are in general throughout our earthly lives to what lies ahead of us. My tragedy was completely unforeseen. I didn't expect it and wasn't prepared for it because I couldn't *see* it coming. This is the reality of our human condition—that we will continue to live each day not knowing what the day may bring, good or bad.

This all sounds a bit depressing, I know, but the good news is that we have a God who does not leave us in the dark. In our grim and dim circumstances, He gives us light, and in our blindness, He leads us.

God says in Isaiah 42:16 (NLT), "I will lead blind Israel down a new path."

The new path that God is likely referencing here is the way, the truth, and the life of Jesus Christ that He will reveal to blind Israel or to those who have not yet known the truth of the gospel. Essentially, He is saying that He will open the eyes of those who don't know Jesus to the light of His saving grace so that they may find their way in and through Him.

The conversion of the apostle Paul is a quite literal example of this:

> Meanwhile, Saul [later given the name Paul] was uttering threats with every breath and was eager to kill the Lord's followers … As he was approaching Damascus on this mission, a light from heaven suddenly shone down around him. He fell to the ground and heard a voice saying to him, "Saul! Saul! Why are you persecuting me?"
>
> "Who are you, lord?" Saul asked.
>
> And the voice replied, "I am Jesus, the one you are persecuting! Now get up and go into the city, and you will be told what you must do."
>
> The men with Saul stood speechless, for they heard the sound of someone's voice but saw no one! Saul picked himself up off the ground, but when he opened his eyes he was blind. So his companions led him by the hand to Damascus. He remained there blind for three days and did not eat or drink. (Acts 9:1, 9:3–9, NLT)

God then speaks to a believer named Ananias and instructs him to go find Saul [Paul] and lay hands on him in order to heal his blindness. The scripture goes on to say,

> So Ananias went and found Saul. He laid his hands on him and said, "Brother Saul, the Lord Jesus, who appeared to you on the road, has sent me so that you might regain your sight and be filled with the Holy Spirit." Instantly something like scales fell

from Saul's eyes, and he regained his sight. Then he got up and was baptized. (Acts 9:17–18, NLT)

And immediately he began preaching about Jesus in the synagogues, saying, "He is indeed the Son of God!"

All who heard him were amazed. "Isn't this the same man who caused such devastation among Jesus' followers in Jerusalem?" they asked. "And didn't he come here to arrest them and take them in chains to the leading priests?"

Saul's preaching became more and more powerful, and the Jews in Damascus couldn't refute his proofs that Jesus was indeed the Messiah. (Acts 9:20–22, NLT)

God did not leave Saul in his physical blindness or spiritual darkness; rather, He *literally* opened his eyes to the power and realness of Jesus Christ showing Him as the only way, truth, and life. Whether we are talking about darkness that is physical or spiritual in nature as in Paul's case or whether it's darkness rooted in grief, anger, fear, or doubt, this same concept holds true: Jesus is the way out of it all.

In John 8:12 (NLT), Jesus said, "I am the light of the world. If you follow me, you won't have to walk in darkness, because you will have the light that leads to life."

The road walked after loss is not an easy one; it's not one that anyone ever wants to travel on—one where the goodness of life can't always be seen beyond it. But if you choose to turn to God rather than turn from Him, He *will* brighten your way and smooth it out before you. God promises his guidance, leadership, and provision to Israel in Isaiah 42:16 (NLT) when He says, "Yes, I will indeed do these things; I will not forsake them."

And He offers all those to us as well as we posture ourselves in a position of dependence on Him.

In the midst of my dark place, I can attest that God gave me glimpses of light that led me. As I couldn't see how I was going to get through what I was facing, I had to rely on God to show me the light that leads to life.

And one step at a time, He did. It wasn't instantaneous, surely wasn't void of pain, and was a process, but I know for a fact that I would still be walking each day in the dark—emotionally, mentally, and certainly spiritually—if it were not for Him.

Losing someone you love is not something that you will ever get *over*. Rather, it is something that you someway, somehow get *through*. And that someway somehow is someone—Jesus. In the midst of your pain and grief, the light of the world, the smoother of roads, and the way, the truth, and the life stands by your side. And He won't leave. Though you walk now in darkness, the Lord will be your light.

Heavenly Father, I desperately need You to brighten the darkness before me and smooth out the road ahead of me. Lord, I know and confess that You are the one true God, the creator of everything. You are the potter and I am the clay. Forgive me for my anger and for speaking of things I know nothing about. Lord, I believe You see the depth of my grief, know how much I love Natalie and Noah, and know how painful it is for me to not have them here anymore. I seek You for help. I put my hope in You, for that is the only place for my hope to be. Please brighten this darkness that I'm facing. Please help me in my suffering and pain and be my light. Lord, You are the Redeemer; please redeem this in my life. Amen.

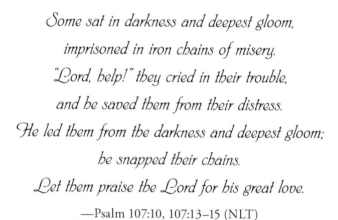

Some sat in darkness and deepest gloom,

imprisoned in iron chains of misery.

"Lord, help!" they cried in their trouble,

and he saved them from their distress.

He led them from the darkness and deepest gloom;

he snapped their chains.

Let them praise the Lord for his great love.

—Psalm 107:10, 107:13–15 (NLT)

CHAPTER 3

GOING PLACES

For the Lord has comforted his people
and will have compassion on them in their suffering.

—Isaiah 49:13 (NLT)

The Lord will comfort Israel again
and have pity on her ruins.
Her desert will blossom like Eden,
her barren wilderness like the garden of the Lord.

—Isaiah 51:3 (NLT)

Grief doesn't feel good. It is debilitating and all-consuming while in the depths of it; often irrational, untimely, and inescapable; and inherently uncomfortable—not only for the griever but also for those around them. It's awkward and sometimes hurtful when people don't know what to say or say the wrong thing. Jason and I had a well-intentioned person tell us, "Eventually you'll be able to move on." Clearly, that person had no understanding of what it's like to lose a baby. It's not something you ever move on from, and it's not something that gets *better* with time. It gets *different* with time, and eventually, you move forward, but you never move on.

It can be hard for others to relate to our grief and understand how to empathize with us. The good news, though, is that while people may disappoint us, God never will. 2 Chronicles 30:9 (NASB) tells us, "For the Lord your God is gracious and compassionate, and will not turn his face away from you if you return to him."

God doesn't look away from the tears falling down our faces because it's not pretty to look at. He doesn't plug His ears when we cry out in grief. He doesn't turn away when we are falling to pieces. Isaiah 30:18 (NASB) also says, "Therefore the Lord longs to be gracious to you, and therefore He waits on high to have compassion on you."

When our lives feel to be in a state of ruin, our Heavenly Father longs to have compassion on us and comfort us—*and that's not all.* His compassion and comfort are typically not passive in nature, but rather transformative in nature.

In Isaiah 51:3 (NLT) as we read at the beginning of the chapter, the prophet Isaiah speaks of the Lord comforting Israel and having pity on her ruins that her desert would blossom like Eden and her barren wilderness like the garden of the Lord. *Desert* and *barren wilderness*—those may feel like accurate descriptors of the places you find yourself in after loss, particularly the loss of a baby or child. The term *barren* depicts emptiness and childlessness. The terms *desert* and *wilderness* depict places that are unknown to you where you may be lost, afraid, and lonely.

But the prophet Isaiah tells us that God does not want to leave us in those places. He wants to pour out His mercy on us and lead us to a place where the mending of our broken hearts can begin—where our desert and barren wilderness begin to look more like a blossoming garden. I realize that may be hard to imagine for your life now, but our God is the transformer of lives. He takes the broken, hopeless, and inconceivable and mends, restores, and works wonders:

This is what God says,
the God who builds a road right through the ocean,
who carves a path through pounding waves …
Be alert, be present. I'm about to do something
brand-new.
It's bursting out! Don't you see it?
There it is! I'm making a road through the desert,
rivers in the badlands.
Wild animals will say 'Thank you!'
—the coyotes and the buzzards—
Because I provided water in the desert,
rivers through the sunbaked earth,
Drinking water for the people I chose,
the people I made especially for myself,
a people custom-made to praise me.

—Isaiah 43:16, 43:19–21 (The Message version)

This truth is also exemplified in Jeremiah 31:13 (NLT), which says, "I will turn their mourning into joy. I will comfort them and exchange their sorrow for rejoicing."

This may have been the most meaningful Bible verse to Jason and me following our losses. It was one that we held on to in the depths of our sorrow—that as hard as it was to imagine at the time, God could somehow give us joy and make us rejoice again.

Although the context of this verse wasn't specifically referring to mourning and sorrow from the loss of a loved one, the concept is still an important one for us. The prophet Jeremiah writes this verse, inspired by God, in reference to the mourning that Israel was experiencing under their exile and captivity. God is speaking here of Israel's liberation and restoration by which He will turn their mourning to joy, comfort them, and make them rejoice.

God gave the Israelites, who were living in a terrifying present of captivity and exile, the promise of a bright future where their lives would no longer be consumed by mourning and sorrow.

Similarly, God knows how to free us from the captivity of our grief. He knows how to make us rejoice after our sorrow. Our present now may be filled with mourning, yes, but through the Lord's transformative compassion, that is not all that lies ahead.

Though your life will never be the same as it was before your loss, if you let God in and let Him work, He will not leave you where you are.

Dear God, thank You that You are my Heavenly Father, that I can come to You like a child coming to her daddy. Thank You for the compassion You have on me in my suffering, that You see me, and offer comfort to me. Lord, I am choosing to trust in You and rely on You as I feel like I am walking in a barren desert. Father, my prayer is that my desert will blossom like Eden and my barren wilderness like the garden of the Lord. Father, I need You for I feel weak. I am looking to You and am trying to do my best day by day, walking in this new scary place without Natalie and Noah. I need You to keep going ahead of me. I need to find strength in You. I miss Natalie and Noah and I am devastated that my future with them is lost, that everything I hoped for with them is gone. But I trust them to You and I trust my life to You. I know they are safe in Your care, and I ask that You would lead me in the safety of Your care as well as I walk each day in this terrifying new place. Amen.

Truly my soul finds rest in God;
my salvation comes from him.
Truly he is my rock and my salvation;
he is my fortress, I will never be shaken.
Yes, my soul, find rest in God;
my hope comes from him.
Truly he is my rock and my salvation;
he is my fortress, I will not be shaken.
My salvation and my honor depend on God;
he is my mighty rock, my refuge.
Trust in him at all times, you people;
pour out your hearts to him,
for God is our refuge.

—Psalm 62:1–2, 62:5–8 (NIV)

CHAPTER 4

The Only One Who Knows

By wisdom the Lord laid the earth's foundations,
by understanding he set the heavens in place;
by his knowledge the watery depths were divided,
and the clouds let drop the dew.

—Proverbs 3:19–20 (NIV)

What is the price of two sparrows—one copper coin?
But not a single sparrow can fall to the ground
without your Father knowing it.
And the very hairs on your head are all numbered.
So don't be afraid;
you are more valuable to God than a whole flock of sparrows.

—Matthew 10:29–33 (NLT)

Why would a loving and good God allow a baby to die? Or a child? Or a father or husband? Or a young woman who has barely experienced life yet? There is no easy answer to this. I realize that this is a hard chapter, friend, so please bear with me. After my losses,

I did a lot of wrestling with God. I remember awakening in the middle of the night and yelling out, "Why, God, why!" I wanted to understand why it happened—why He had allowed something so horrific and so painful in my life. Maybe you too are familiar with this kind of wrestling.

It's OK to ask God those hard questions. It's OK to struggle with Him, and we see that in the life of Jacob in Genesis 32. In this chapter, Jacob and his family flee from his uncle Laban's land and begin to journey back to Jacob's hometown. Jacob had been estranged from his brother Esau, and he fears that reuniting with him in their homeland will not be a friendly encounter. In an attempt to appease him, Jacob sends messengers ahead with a gift to Esau. When the messengers return, they tell Jacob that Esau is on his way to meet him along with four hundred men. For seemingly good reason, Jacob is fearful and splits up his family into two separate herds in the hopes that if one group fell victim to Esau's men, the other may escape.

Jacob then prays for God's help, sends even more gifts ahead to Esau, hoping to pacify him, and finally sends his wives, children, and all his possessions across the River Jabbok. He then spends the night alone in the wilderness, where he is visited by a stranger—later realized to be God Himself—who wrestles with him throughout the entire night. At the very end of their wrestling, the stranger, God, wrenches Jacob's hip, essentially crippling him. Even then, Jacob holds on and says, "I will not let you go unless you bless me" (Genesis 32:26).

This is the first takeaway from Jacob's story: *he holds on.* He doesn't let go of God or turn away or run from Him. As Jacob struggles with God, *he holds on to Him.*

God then gives Jacob a new name, saying, "Your name will no longer be Jacob, but Israel, because you have struggled with God and with humans and have overcome" (Genesis 32:28). This name Israel is thought to have meant "he struggles with God." What a fitting name, right? He *literally* wrestled with God.

Jacob's fight with God doesn't sound like it was a pleasant experience: he surely did not sleep the entire night and was left limping from the blow to his hip. But through his struggle, he sees God, experiences Him in a tangible way, and is touched by Him. Genesis 32:30 (NLT) tells us,

> Jacob named the place Peniel (which means "face of God"), for he said, "I have seen God face to face, yet my life has been spared."

Our struggle with God is not likely to be a literal one as it was for Jacob, but it is a struggle nonetheless. It's a struggle of questions, doubts, anger, confusion, and fear. But just as it was for Jacob, in our wrestling we *face* God. And in the midst of it, if we can hold on as Jacob did, God will manifest Himself and minister to us.

In Genesis 32:29, I find it interesting that Jacob pointedly asks God a question:

> "Please tell me your name," Jacob said. "Why do you want to know my name?" the man replied. Then he blessed Jacob there.

Jacob asks God a question: he asks Him what His name is. But God does not give Jacob an answer. Jacob is given a blessing, but not an answer. I think the same concept often holds true for us as we question the circumstances we are facing.

In all my wrestling and questioning of God, I never got a finite answer to the "why" I was seeking. But as I faced Him and held on to Him through it, I realized that rather than seeking to know the answers to all my questions, I should be seeking to know more of God Himself. And as my perspective changed to that in the midst of my wrestling, I came to learn and submit to a very important truth:

That God is sovereign—He is in control over all, even when painful and tragic things happen.

And He is loving—He is good, kind, merciful, and full of compassion, even when painful and tragic things happen.

It's not that He at some moments is sovereign and at other times, loving; rather, He is simultaneously and continuously both of those things even when circumstances may not seem to align with that truth.

I understand God's sovereignty to mean that He is the Almighty. He is ruler over all. He is the ultimate authority and has supreme power. Jeremiah 10:12–13 (NIV) tells us,

> But God made the earth by his power;
> he founded the world by his wisdom
> and stretched out the heavens by his understanding.
> When he thunders, the waters in the heavens roar;
> he makes clouds rise from the ends of the earth.
> He sends lightning with the rain
> and brings out the wind from his storehouses.

It seems that often in God's sovereignty, He *allows* things to happen that we don't understand. There is so much that goes on in the heavenly realms that is far beyond our awareness. There are spiritual forces at work that we cannot see (Ephesians 6:12), there is an evil one who roams around like a lion looking for someone to devour (1 Peter 5:8), and we live in a fallen world that has succumbed to the effects of sin (Genesis 3:17–19). The recognition of the absolute sovereignty of God is not reason to blame Him for the tragedies in life; rather, it is reason to surrender to His ultimate knowing and our lack thereof.

And this reality of God's sovereignty does not negate the fact that He is a loving and good God:

> For his unfailing love toward those who fear him is
> as great as the height of the heavens above the earth.
> (Psalm 103:11, NLT)

> For God so loved the world that he gave his one
> and only Son, that whoever believes in him shall
> not perish but have eternal life. (John 3:16, NIV)

> We know how much God loves us, and we have put
> our trust in his love. God is love, and all who live
> in love live in God, and God lives in them. (1 John
> 4:16, NLT)

God *is* love. He isn't just loving, doesn't just show love; He *is* love. The juxtaposition of God's sovereignty and love can be seen in John 11 through the death of Lazarus. Jesus is told that Lazarus, whom He loves, is sick, yet He stays where He is for two more days rather than going to see or heal Lazarus. After those two days, He tells His disciples that they all should travel back to Judea and that Lazarus had died. How did He know that he had died? Because He is all-knowing.

When Jesus is met at separate times by Lazarus's sisters, Martha and Mary, both of their first words to Jesus are "Lord, if you had been here, my brother would not have died" (John 11:21, 11:32). This was the reality—Jesus allowed Lazarus to die. After Jesus is met by Mary with this statement, we read:

> When Jesus saw her weeping, and the Jews who had
> come along with her also weeping, he was deeply
> moved in spirit and troubled. "Where have you laid
> him?" he asked. "Come and see, Lord," they replied.
> Jesus wept. (John 11:33–35, NIV)

Jesus wept. The king of the universe wept.

He then goes on right after that to resurrect Lazarus from the dead, which He *knew* all along that He was going to do. So why would He be so deeply moved in spirit and troubled and weeping? I think probably from seeing the pain and grief being experienced by those He loved at Lazarus's graveside. In His love for Martha, Mary, and whoever else was there, He was so grieved by their anguish that He literally wept.

His sovereignty does not negate His love.

Now for most all of us, Jesus is not likely to literally resurrect our loved ones from the dead in the here and now as He did Lazarus, but even so, the certainty of God's sovereignty and love can keep us grounded as we wrestle through the whys of our circumstances.

For me personally, I had to work through my questions, doubts, and confusion and come to a place where I was able to submit to God as sovereign Lord and loving Father in the midst of my suffering, even without having been given the answer to my why. It wasn't easy, and it didn't come naturally, but it enabled me to not remain utterly tormented by the why as I surrendered it all to Him.

We don't know and can't know so much in these earthly lives we live. But what we can do in all of our unknowing is fall at the feet of Jesus and decide to trust Him even through anger, questions, and doubts. It's OK to grapple through the hard questions, yes, and it's best to hold on to Him as you do.

Journal entry from July 1, 2017

Heavenly Father, my understanding is so limited, and I know there is no use trying to reason and figure everything out. But, Lord, I'm just in pain and I want to understand. Forgive me, Father, for my questioning, my doubting, my confusion. I know Your ways are higher than mine and Your thoughts are far higher than mine. I know that You see the big picture, while all I see is through the tiny lens of my grief. Lord, I need You. I want to experience You, feel Your presence, and know You more. Lord, I am seeking You day by day, and day by day, I'm seeking Your will. Father, I want to see this redeemed in my life. I believe You're working; I just can't seem to see it right now. Lord, I choose to trust You. I believe You have plans for my future, and I believe You work all things for the good of those who love You and are called according to Your purposes. All my fears I lay at Your feet. Father, I need Your grace and mercy for I am weak and frail. Thank You for Natalie and Noah and that they're in heaven with You. I can't wait to see them. I hope they know how much their mommy loves them. O Lord, help me today. I love You. Amen.

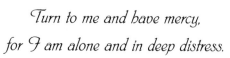

Turn to me and have mercy,
for I am alone and in deep distress.

—Psalm 25:16 (NLT)

CHAPTER 5

IN NEED OF A LIFT

In all their suffering he also suffered,
and he personally rescued them.
In His love and mercy He redeemed them.
He lifted them up and carried them through the years.

—Isaiah 63:9 (NLT)

After losing Natalie and Noah, one of my biggest challenges was figuring out how to live again—not in a physical sense, but in the sense of how to start living my life again without them here. In a lot of ways, I didn't want to. I wanted to curl up in a ball on the floor in their empty room and just stay there. And I did that, a lot.

I didn't think at first that I would want or be able to go into their room. I thought that it would be too painful to be in there. But the very first time I stepped foot in my house upon arriving home from the hospital, it was the very first place that I went. I remember walking up the stairs, turning down the hallway, opening the door to their room, and laying myself down on the carpet in there, just sobbing. I felt drawn to that room and ended up spending most of my time there in the weeks following their loss. Crying, thinking, praying, mourning—all while just lying on the floor.

If it weren't for God lifting me up and carrying me through those weeks and months, I might have stayed there indefinitely. I didn't have it in me to stand up, pull myself together, and live each day as I knew I'd been called to live. I couldn't do it on my own, and thank God that I didn't have to.

Isaiah 63:9 implies that God doesn't just sympathize with our suffering, He actually suffers *with* us. It's as if He doesn't just see our distress and feel pity for us; He sees us and joins us in our suffering. Whether it's on the floor in our empty nurseries or wherever else you find yourself most often, He is there with us and feels our pain too.

We can see this exemplified in Judges 10 (NLT):

> For eighteen years [the Philistines and Ammonites] oppressed all the Israelites east of the Jordan River in the land of the Amorites (that is, in Gilead). The Ammonites also crossed to the west side of the Jordan and attacked Judah, Benjamin, and Ephraim. *The Israelites were in great distress* [emphasis mine]. Finally, they cried out to the Lord for help, saying, "We have sinned against you because we have abandoned you as our God and have served the images of Baal" ... Then the Israelites put aside their foreign gods and served the Lord. *And he was grieved by their misery* [emphasis mine]. (Judges 10:8–10, 10:16)

The Israelites were in great distress, and He was grieved by their misery. Could this not also read, I, Lindsay, was in great distress, and He was grieved by my misery; and *you* were in great distress, and He was grieved by your misery. Our suffering grieves Him, and to be grieved is to suffer. In all their suffering He also suffered; in all our suffering He also suffers.

And yet, He doesn't only suffer with us. As also indicated in Isaiah 63:9 and portrayed in Judges 11 (NLT), He rescues us:

> The Ammonites began their war against Israel …
> So Jephthah led his army against the Ammonites,
> *and the Lord gave him victory* [emphasis mine]. He
> crushed the Ammonites, devastating about twenty
> towns from Aroer to an area near Minnith and
> as far away as Abel-keramim. In this way Israel
> defeated the Ammonites. (Judges 11:4, 11:32–33)

The Israelites were in great distress, He was grieved by their misery, and the Lord gave them victory. The Lord did for them what they could not do for themselves. And that is exactly what He does for us too, just in a different context. When we don't have the strength or even the desire to pick ourselves up off the floor (literally speaking as in my case), He comes to lift us up. When we don't know how we're ever going to be able to start walking through our lives again, He carries us through. The Lord says in Isaiah 46:4 (NLT), "I made you, and I will care for you. I will carry you along and save you."

After experiencing loss, figuring out how to live again doesn't happen overnight. It's a process and it takes time. And most importantly, it's not something that you have to do on your own. Just as a father carries his child when the child is too tired or weak to walk on their own, so will your Heavenly Father do for you.

Journal entry from July 2, 2017

Heavenly Father, You are my Father and I am so in need of that relationship. I need to experience, feel, and fully believe in Your love. Help me to do that. Lord, I seek You and I need You to rescue me, to redeem me in Your love and mercy, to lift me up and carry me. I'm scared, Lord, of everything going back to "normal," and maybe I shouldn't be. But, Lord, without Natalie and Noah, nothing seems normal. It is starting to feel like—or I'm starting to see how—things could go back to how it was before You gave them life, but that just feels so wrong because they did have life and they were here. Lord, I know that You give and take away, and still, Father, blessed be Your name. My hope and trust are in You and You alone because everything else in this life is uncertain, impermanent, and fading. I'm trying, Lord. I'm really trying, but I feel weak and just like a scared little girl. I feel like I'm asking a lot from You. Please have mercy on me. Lord, I need Your strength and Your spirit. I ask and pray that You, my redeemer, would redeem this in my life and would restore my life. I want to walk in Your will and nothing else. I don't want to be apart from You or outside Your hand. Help me, Lord. Amen.

*As I sit here in this tearstained rocking chair,
looking at two empty cradles with empty
arms and an empty tummy,
I choose to look up. I choose to believe in
the One who gives and takes away.
Blessed be the name of the Lord!*

CHAPTER 6

DEFIANT PRAISE

The Lord gave me what I had,
and the Lord has taken it away.
Praise the name of the Lord!

—Job 1:21 (NLT)

The very first place I started reading in the Bible following my losses was Job. I was drawn to his story because I could, for the first time, relate to it in a sense. I was desperate to find any kind of encouragement or hope from it. And I did, but even more than that, I found myself challenged by it.

The book of Job tells us that Job lost all ten of his children, all his possessions were destroyed, and he became ailed with painful sores from the soles of his feet to the crown of his head. To me, this sounds like the epitome of suffering.

We read in Job 1 (NLT) when a messenger comes to tell Job that all his children have died:

> Job stood up and tore his robe in grief. Then he shaved his head and *fell to the ground to worship* [emphasis mine]. He said, "I came naked from my

mother's womb, and I will be naked when I leave. The Lord gave me what I had, and the Lord has taken it away. Praise the name of the Lord!" (Job 1:20–21)

Later on in Job 2 (NLT), we also read,

> So Satan left the Lord's presence, and he struck Job with terrible boils from head to foot. Job scraped his skin with a piece of broken pottery as he sat among the ashes. His wife said to him, "Are you still trying to maintain your integrity? Curse God and die." But Job replied, "You talk like a foolish woman. Should we accept only good things from the hand of God and never anything bad?" So in all this, Job said nothing wrong. (Job 2:7–10)

It was not because Job was unmoved by his circumstances that he was able to maintain his integrity. When three of his friends come to console him, Job 2:13 tells us,

> They sat on the ground with him for seven days and nights. No one said a word to Job, for they saw that his suffering was too great for words.

And when Job speaks for the first time to his friends, he says,

> I cannot eat for sighing; my groans pour out like water. What I always feared has happened to me. What I dreaded has come true. I have no peace, no quietness. I have no rest; only trouble comes. (Job 3:24–26, NLT)

It's also not that Job didn't question God or wrestle through what had happened to him, because he did. He questioned God, *a lot*. Job questioned why he was even born (Job 3:11), why he was a target for suffering (Job 7:20, NLT), and goes on in Job 10:3–6 (NLT) to say to God,

> What do you gain by oppressing me? Why do you reject me, the work of your own hands, while smiling on the schemes of the wicked? Are your eyes like those of a human? Do you see things only as people see them? Is your lifetime only as long as ours? Is your life so short that you must quickly probe for my guilt and search for my sin?

Talk about being frank with God, right? He challenges God and expresses his feelings awfully bluntly to Him, *but* he doesn't curse Him or discount his belief in Him. Despite his great suffering, lack of understanding, confusion, and anger, in Job 42:1–6 (NLT) we see him confessing God's sovereign rule over his life and even repenting for having questioned Him.

This serves as a challenge to you and me today. Will we follow Job's example and praise even when we're hurting, believe even when it doesn't make sense, and confess who God is even through our questions?

We may have days when this feels harder to do than others. Grief is like that—it comes in waves. We can have moments when the depths of pain and panic feel absolutely debilitating to where the proclamation of praise feels nearly impossible. It's more than OK to be honest with God about our feelings, which are at times uncontrollable.

But the *choice* that we have in the midst of our feelings is controllable. We have the choice to curse and blame God or to defiantly proclaim trust and hope in Him in the midst of our devastations.

I made my choice to do the latter all those years ago, and it was one of the best things I've ever done. Choosing to still praise God and trust Him doesn't invalidate the extent of our suffering. Rather, it validates who God is in the midst of our suffering. It proclaims that God is the Lord of our lives even when our lives have fallen to pieces.

Our offering of praise to God should not be conditional on our circumstances. He is worthy of our praise because of who He is, not because of what He gives us. Like Job, can we praise the name of the Lord even in our grief today? May we not let the tears falling down our faces keep us from doing so.

Journal entry from July 3, 2017

Heavenly Father, yesterday was a horrible day. I felt depressed and dark and mad and a little hopeless. I need Your help so desperately. I'm in so much pain and I'm so confused. I miss Natalie and Noah. Father, You know how much I wanted an earthly life here with them. I can't understand why or how this happened, and all I can do is fall on to You and Your word and Your promises. If I don't, I will fall flat on my face. Lord, each day I am making a conscious decision to trust You and hope in You. I know my feelings don't always match up with that, but that is my heart. Lord, if I didn't choose to trust You, what would I do? The uncertainties of life are far too scary and daunting to handle on my own. Lord, You know me and I have to believe that You are working things for my good and that I am in Your hand like clay in a potter's hand. Lord, in this time of deep pain and fear, I need to know You more. I need to find You, see You, hear You, and experience You. Help me to do that. Father, You know what I need right now better than I do. You are the Redeemer, and I continue to hope and believe that You are redeeming this in my life. Father, I need Your restoration. I'm trying to walk day by day, and it's hard. I want to honor You and please You with my faith and hope. I'm trying, Lord, and I believe, but help my unbelief. Amen.

"Worthy of My Song (Worthy of It All)"
Maverick City Music (feat. Phil Wickham and Chandler Moore)

I'm gonna sing 'til my heart starts changing
Oh, I'm gonna worship 'til I mean every word
'Cause the way I feel and the fear I'm facing
Doesn't change who You are or what You deserve
I give You my worship
You still deserve it
You're worthy, You're worthy
You're worthy of my song
I'll pour out Your praises
In blessing and breaking
You're worthy, You're worthy
You're worthy of my song
Yes, You are, yes, You are, Jesus
You're worthy
I'm gonna live like my King is risen
Gonna preach to my soul that You've already won
And even though I can't see it, I'm gonna keep believing
That every promise You make is as good as done
I give You my worship
You still deserve it
You're worthy, You're worthy
You're worthy of my song
I'll pour out Your praises
In blessing and breaking
You're worthy, You're worthy
Jesus, You're worthy of my song
You're worthy, You're worthy
Jesus, You're worthy of my song
You're worthy, oh, You're worthy
When I sat by that hospital bed, You were worthy
And she could barely lift her head, You were worthy

After all those tears were shed, You were worthy
I'll never stop singing Your praise
I'll never stop singing Your praise
And in the blessing, in the pain, You are worthy
Whether You say yes or no or wait, You are worthy
Through it all, I choose to say, "You are worthy"
I'll never stop singing Your praise
No, I'll never stop singing Your praise
And when I finally see Your face, I'll cry worthy
And when You wipe these tears away, I'll cry worthy
Above every other name, You are worthy
I'll never stop singing Your praise
No, I'll never stop singing Your praise
I'll never stop singing Your praise
I'll never stop singing Your praise
I give You my worship
'Cause You still deserve it
You're worthy, You're worthy
Jesus, You're worthy of my song
I'll pour out Your praises
In blessing and breaking
You're worthy, You're worthy
Jesus, You're worthy of my song

CHAPTER 7

THE FORMING
OF PEARLS

And we know that God causes everything to work together
for the good of those who love God
and are called according to his purpose for them.

—Romans 8:28 (NLT)

For it is God who works in you to will and to act
in order to fulfill his good purpose.

—Philippians 2:13 (NIV)

Did you know that pearls are formed when an irritant, some kind of foreign substance, gets into an oyster's shell? In an attempt to protect itself, the oyster covers the irritant with layers of a substance that ultimately transforms it into a beautiful pearl. Pearls don't begin as pearls. Rather, they start as unwanted, potentially harmful irritants that are turned into something valuable.

The loss of a baby or someone we love is certainly more than just an irritant in our lives, but I hope you can see the symbolism. Just as the irritant isn't simply discarded by the oyster but rather is formed into something new, the same can be true for our pain. It does not have to be wasted and worthless; pain will always hurt, yes, but it also can have a purpose.

God can take devastation and eventually extract value from it. It can be nearly impossible at times to imagine that this holds true for our situations, I know, but it is the truth of what God can do and of who He is.

This concept is exemplified in the life of Joseph starting in Genesis 37. A quick recap of Joseph's story is as follows: Joseph had ten half brothers, all of whom hated him and were jealous of him. They intended to kill him but ended up selling him into slavery instead when he was just seventeen years old. The traders he was sold to took him from his homeland to Egypt, where they sold him to a man named Potiphar who was an officer of Pharaoh. Joseph served in Potiphar's household for an unknown amount of time before being wrongfully accused of inappropriate conduct toward Potiphar's wife and thrown into prison. Joseph spent thirteen years total between his time serving in Potiphar's house and being in prison.

Thirteen years. I wonder what his state of mind was like during those thirteen years. Did he feel discouraged, disappointed, and disheartened? I would imagine so. Did he feel hopeless about his circumstances? Maybe. Did he believe that God could redeem all those lost years, the suffering he experienced, and the heartache he endured? I don't know the answer to that, but I do know that Genesis 39:20–21 (NLT) tells us, "there [Joseph] remained. But the Lord was with Joseph in the prison and showed him his faithful love."

After those thirteen years, Joseph—being God-gifted with the ability to interpret dreams—was brought before Pharaoh, where he interpreted two of Pharaoh's disturbing dreams. Pharaoh was so impressed and pleased with Joseph that he made him ruler over all of Egypt, holding a rank higher than anyone else except for Pharaoh himself. For the next seven years, Joseph served in this high position, facilitating the storage of extra food in anticipation of a savage, seven-year-long famine expected to come after seven years of plenty.

When the famine begins, it affects the surrounding countries and eventually Egypt as well. Food becomes scarce everywhere *except* for the storehouses Joseph had built. People from all over travel to Egypt to buy food from Joseph—including Joseph's brothers who, all those years ago, had attempted to hurt him.

After his brothers discover that this ruler of Egypt who was in charge of any and all food distribution was in fact their brother Joseph, they were quite surprised (to say the least) and feared (reasonably so) retribution. But rather than Joseph engaging in retaliation against them, Joseph forgives them and demonstrates a rational and admirable perspective on all the bad that happened to him. To his brothers' fear, Genesis 50:19–21 (MSG) says,

> Joseph replied, "Don't be afraid. Do I act for God? Don't you see, *you planned evil against me but God used those same plans for my good* [emphasis mine], as you see all around you right now—life for many people. Easy now, you have nothing to fear; I'll take care of you and your children." He reassured them, speaking with them heart-to-heart.

Joseph faced bad circumstances, but God *used* those bad circumstances and made them have significance and purpose. He took the irritant, lightly speaking, in Joseph's life and made it into a pearl. Joseph suffered, and God didn't waste it. Through it all, God was *with* Joseph, and through it all, God *worked*.

While I'm not sure how Joseph felt in the midst of all of the bad he faced, I know that after my losses I couldn't imagine how *anything* could be good again. I couldn't understand how God could redeem, exchange, or use it. But I didn't need to see it or understand it. All I needed to do was trust that He could.

Almost six years later, I can tell you that He did. He has given me many opportunities to minister to other women who have experienced loss, He has given me a passion and ultimately a vocation for encouraging women who are suffering, and He has given me three children since then to live with me here on earth.

It's not by any means that my pain is gone, because it's certainly not. I still desperately miss Natalie and Noah. I still cry, but my life now is no longer paralyzed by the pain. He and He alone has added value, purpose, joy, rejoicing, and good to my life in ways I never thought possible after the extent of my anguish and brokenness following my losses.

While grief may cloud our ability to see any good in our tomorrows, belief in God's redeeming nature can sustain us despite our lack of vision.

Will you choose today to believe that God can take something so broken, so devastating, so heart-shattering, and somehow use it? Even though believing that doesn't make dealing with loss any less painful, it can give you an anchor to hold on to in your darkest hours.

Journal entry from July 4, 2017

Heavenly Father, it's another day. I still often can't believe that this is my life right now. That Natalie and Noah are gone and they're not coming back. Father, what do I do now without them? Lord, I need a vision from You. I need to hear from You. I believe in Your word, that You cause everything to work together for the good of those who love God and are called according to Your purpose for them. Father, I have to believe that You are using this in my life. That You have purposes and plans I cannot see. That You have hope and good for my future. Lord, I say again, I believe, but help my unbelief. The future seems scary and unclear now. I am looking to You and relying on You. I give You my fears. I know that the love I felt holding Natalie and Noah in my arms is just a fraction of the love You have for me and for them. Lord, You are God and You are my Father, and I come to You as Your daughter professing that I need You. I am weak and tired, and I miss my babies. Though I cannot feel it or see it, I believe that You love me and have good for me. Please help me to feel it and see it. Help me to know You more and experience You more. Father, You know the desires and longings of my heart, and I trust those to You. May Your will be done in my life here on earth as it is in heaven. Amen.

He heals the brokenhearted and bandages their wounds ...
the Lord's delight is in those who fear him,
those who put their hope in his unfailing love.

—Psalm 147:3, 147:11 (NLT)

CHAPTER 8

UNSHAKABLE (EVEN IF)

If we are thrown into the blazing furnace,
the God whom we serve is able to save us.
He will rescue us from your power, Your Majesty.
But even if he doesn't,
we want to make it clear to you, Your Majesty,
that we will never serve your gods
or worship the gold statue you have set up.

—Daniel 3:17–18 (NLT)

The story of Shadrach, Meshach, and Abednego has always stood out to me. If you're not familiar with it or need a quick recap, King Nebuchadnezzar made a large gold statue and issued a decree stating that all people needed to bow to the statue or else be thrown into a blazing furnace. Despite this decree, Shadrach, Meshach, and Abednego refuse to bow to the statue even while knowing the consequence of their decision. They tell King Nebuchadnezzar, as we read in Daniel 3:17–18, that if they are thrown into the blazing furnace, their God is able to save them, but even if he doesn't, they will never bow down.

Their resolve and commitment to God is extraordinary. In the face of certain death, they remain steadfast in their faith and service to God alone. *Even if he doesn't*—this proclamation may be the greatest evidence of unshakeable faith.

This has been my heart's cry to God. Through years of infertility and a deep desire for children, my prayers for so many years involved earnest petitions for children born through my womb followed by "but even if you don't, I will still love you and serve you."

Do you know the saying "don't talk the talk unless you can walk the walk"? Well, after I lost Natalie and Noah, I was faced with having to walk the walk. I had to decide if I really and truly meant all the times I professed to God, "But even if you don't." In the face of the deepest pain I've ever experienced and may ever experience, I had to decide whether my faith in God was going to waver or whether I was going to stand by my word.

As Shadrach, Meshach, and Abednego were led to the blazing furnace, I imagine they faced that same decision as well. As they got closer to the flames and could feel the burn of the heat, were they going to change their minds and bow to the statue?

They didn't. And metaphorically speaking, neither did I.

Shadrach, Meshach, and Abednego were in fact thrown into the blazing furnace, which, to make matters worse, had been heated seven times hotter than normal. And then, God intervened. Daniel 3:24–25 (NLT) says,

> But suddenly, Nebuchadnezzar jumped up in amazement and exclaimed to his advisers, "Didn't we tie up three men and throw them into the furnace?"
>
> "Yes, Your Majesty, we certainly did," they replied.
>
> "Look!" Nebuchadnezzar shouted. "I see four men, unbound, walking around in the fire unharmed! And the fourth looks like a god!"

God was *with them* in the fire, and He is *with us* in our fires as well.

When we demonstrate that same resolve that Shadrach, Meshach, and Abednego had to remain steadfast in our faith no matter what we're facing, God steps in. He may not immediately rescue us from what we're facing, but He will be with us.

David depicts this truth in his writing of Psalm 23 (NIV):

> The Lord is my shepherd, I lack nothing.
>   He makes me lie down in green pastures,
> he leads me beside quiet waters,
>   he refreshes my soul.
> He guides me along the right paths
>   for his name's sake.
> Even though I walk
>   through the darkest valley,
> I will fear no evil,
>   *for you are with me* [emphasis mine];
> your rod and your staff,
>   they comfort me.
> You prepare a table before me
>   in the presence of my enemies.
> You anoint my head with oil;
>   my cup overflows.
> Surely your goodness and love will follow me
>   all the days of my life,
> and I will dwell in the house of the Lord
>   forever.

I find it interesting that David doesn't say, "*I will not* walk through the darkest valley" or "*if I* walk through the darkest valley"; he says, "*even though* I walk through the darkest valley, I will fear no evil, for you are with me." He does not profess that walking with

God means that we will not walk through dark valleys; rather, he avows that as we do walk through them, God is with us.

As you continue to process your grief and walk through your dark valley, know that the Lord is always with you. He is right beside you. May you remain unshaken.

Heavenly Father, I seek You and I need You. Please give me wisdom as I continue to process through my grief and pain over losing Natalie and Noah. Father, I know that they are safe with You in the heavenly places, and I am thankful for the peace that brings, but it doesn't take away or even reduce the pain and sorrow of losing them here in this earthly life where I am. Father, I want to see Your purposes in this, but even if I don't, I will believe and trust in Your ways that are so much higher than mine because blessed are those who believe without seeing. Forgive me for my lack of understanding and for saying things I know nothing about. I am just a mom who desperately loves and misses her babies. Please give me sensitive ears to hear You and keen eyes to see You through this. I want to know You deeply and walk closely with You all the days of my life. Please have mercy on me, Lord, for I am weak, yet in my weakness, You are my strength. Amen.

I know the Lord is always with me.
I will not be shaken,
for he is right beside me.

—Psalm 16:8 (NLT)

CHAPTER 9

YET AND BUT

I am worn out from sobbing.
All night I flood my bed with weeping,
drenching it with my tears.

—Psalm 6:6 (NLT)

Yet I still belong to you; you hold my right hand.
You guide me with your counsel, leading me to a glorious destiny.
Whom have I in heaven but you? I desire
you more than anything on earth.
My health may fail, and my spirit may grow weak,
but God remains the strength of my heart; he is mine forever.

—Psalm 73:23–26 (NLT)

In Psalm 73, we see the author, Asaph, confessing his feelings of bitterness and envy toward the wicked people whom he saw prospering. His struggle with this almost resulted in him losing faith in God. While the circumstance Asaph was facing is different from the one you and I are facing, I find this psalm to be impactful: "Yet I still belong to you" and "but God remains." These truths written by Asaph hold relevance to us in the aftermath of our losses.

The first is relevant to the wide array of ugly emotions we experience aside from sadness—all those feelings that in some way express a sense of defiance to our circumstances or even to God. Have you ever felt like you wanted to throw a temper tantrum? I did. I wanted to jump up and down and scream at the top of my lungs because I didn't want my circumstances to be what they were.

I *wanted* the babies I was holding to have breath in them.

I *wanted* to take them home with me from the hospital.

I *wanted* to raise them, to go through life with them.

I *wanted* them.

It *was not* fair!

Loss isn't fair—it's true. It's beyond our control, unwanted, and undeserved, but for so many of us in this life, it is a reality.

Anger, fear, and doubt are normal emotional responses to suffering. Yet even as we process all these feelings, Asaph reminds us that we are still His.

I may feel like questioning at times, *yet I still belong to you.*

I may feel like throwing a temper tantrum in defiance of my circumstances, *yet I still belong to you.*

I may feel angry, *yet I still belong to you.*

I may feel like a piece of me is gone, *yet I still belong to you.*

I may feel absolutely exhausted from my grief, *yet I still belong to you.*

Our emotional responses will never be too ugly for Him, and the apostle Paul assures us that nothing will ever separate us from God's love—from being His. Romans 8:31-39 (NLT) says,

> What shall we say about such wonderful things as these? If God is for us, who can ever be against us? Since he did not spare even his own Son but gave him up for us all, won't he also give us everything else? Who dares accuse us whom God has chosen for his own? No one—for God himself has given us right standing with himself. Who then will

condemn us? No one—*for Christ Jesus died for us and was raised to life for us, and he is sitting in the place of honor at God's right hand, pleading for us* [emphasis mine].

Can anything ever separate us from Christ's love? Does it mean he no longer loves us if we have trouble or calamity, or are persecuted, or hungry, or destitute, or in danger, or threatened with death? (As the scriptures say, "For your sake we are killed every day; we are being slaughtered like sheep.") No, despite all these things, overwhelming victory is ours through Christ, who loved us.

And I am convinced that nothing can ever separate us from God's love. Neither death nor life, neither angels nor demons, *neither our fears for today nor our worries about tomorrow—not even the powers of hell can separate us from God's love* [emphasis mine]. No power in the sky above or in the earth below— indeed, nothing in all creation will ever be able to separate us from the love of God that is revealed in Christ Jesus our Lord.

Despite the dire circumstances we face and despite our transient, fleshly feelings of rebellion, Christ Jesus died for us, was raised to life for us, and loves us. And it is our steadfast belief in those facts that enables us to proclaim, "Yet I still belong to you."

The second truth that Asaph highlights in Psalm 73, "but God remains," I find relevant to the effects of our loss. Losing a baby or someone we love touches every part of our lives—it changes *everything*. After losing Natalie and Noah, for a long time, it was hard to enjoy *anything*. Smiling felt so wrong. Laughing felt like a sin. Any and all excitement about tomorrow disappeared.

It's not hard for a despondent demeanor to develop following a loss and when it feels like we've lost so much. That is why actively challenging our perspective is so utterly important, because if we don't, we risk walking through the rest of our lives bitter, cynical, and void of joy. Yes, we have lost *so much*—the person or persons who died, our expectations and hopes for our futures, our sense of joy, our lives as we knew them—all lost.

But God remains.

My world may have fallen to pieces, *but God remains* the rock of my life.

My future expectations may have been shattered, *but God remains* in control of it all.

My faith may have been tested, *but God remains* my hope.

My heart may have been broken, *but God remains* my strength.

Even when it feels like we've lost everything, we still have everything if we have Him. David illustrates this truth in his writing of Psalm 16. David too experienced profound loss in his life—hunted by Saul, who was trying to kill him, he was forced to flee to the woods, hills, and fields to hide, thereby leaving everything familiar and comfortable. With him were four hundred men; with Saul, three thousand. He knew what it was like to have his world fall apart around him, and yet in the midst of it, he writes this in Psalm 16 (GNT):

> Protect me, O God; I trust in you for safety.
> I say to the Lord, "You are my Lord;
>   all the good things I have come from you."
> *You, Lord, are all I have,*
>   *and you give me all I need* [emphasis mine];
>   my future is in your hands.
> How wonderful are your gifts to me;
>   how good they are!
> I praise the Lord, because he guides me,
>   and in the night my conscience warns me.

I am always aware of the Lord's presence;
  he is near, and nothing can shake me.
And so I am thankful and glad,
  and I feel completely secure,
because you protect me from the power of death.
I have served you faithfully,
  and you will not abandon me to the world of the dead.
You will show me the path that leads to life;
  your presence fills me with joy
  and brings me pleasure forever.

I don't know about you, but this challenges me: to be able to say like David, and to mean it, in the face of all we've lost, "You, Lord, are all I have, and you give me all I need."

These are hard concepts, I know, but my prayer is that in whatever you are facing today, you remember that you *are His* and *He is* your greatest need.

Journal entry from July 6, 2017

Father, I want my babies back. I know I can't, but I want them. I don't feel good this morning and feel like I can't handle much. I desperately need Your strength because I feel so weak today. I feel like I've lost so much … but I know, God, if nothing else, You remain. I need to will my mind into that perspective this morning—that in the midst of my loss, You are still with me and You are what I need. Amen.

My eyes are blinded by my tears.
Each day I beg for your help, O Lord;
I lift my hands to you for mercy.

—Psalm 88:9 (NLT)

CHAPTER 10

SEE YOU SOON

So we don't look at the troubles we can see now;
rather, we fix our gaze on things that cannot be seen.
For the things we see now will soon be gone,
but the things we cannot see will last forever.

—2 Corinthians 4:18 (NLT)

And now, dear brothers and sisters, we want you to know
what will happen to the believers who have died so you
will not grieve like people who have no hope. For since we
believe that Jesus died and was raised to life again, we also
believe that when Jesus returns, God will bring back with
him the believers who have died. We tell you this directly
from the Lord: We who are still living when the Lord
returns will not meet him ahead of those who have died.

—1 Thessalonians 4:13–15 (NLT)

When we say goodbye to someone, it signifies that the person is
leaving or that we are leaving that person. It represents the end of
time spent with someone. Goodbyes are a mundane part of life in
a lot of ways. We say goodbye every day to our spouses when they

leave for work or to friends after a get-together is over. These kinds of goodbyes typically are not emotionally charged because we assume that we are going to see the other person again reasonably soon. On the other hand, if we knew that we were never going to see the other person again, saying goodbye to them would look very different.

Saying goodbye to Natalie and Noah's physical bodies was the hardest, most painful thing I've ever had to do. When their bodies were taken, it just about broke me. If you have been through a similar experience, I would imagine that resonates with you. Or maybe you never got the chance to say goodbye in a physical sense. Maybe you never got to see their physical bodies. Even if that was the case, you still had to say goodbye when they left you—and that kind of goodbye is surely just as painful.

These moments in our lives are so anguishing because we truly are saying goodbye forever to those we have lost in this earthly life. It's true that on this side of heaven, we will never physically have them with us or see them again. There is a permanence to that fact that is cause for the extent of agony to those goodbyes.

But thank God that our goodbyes do not have to end there! We have the assured hope that if we have lost a baby or if we have lost anyone who had faith in Christ Jesus, we will see them again. The Bible gives us reassurance of this in 1 Thessalonians 4:13–15 as we read at the beginning of the chapter, and in 2 Samuel when David and Bathsheba lost their infant son. In 2 Samuel 12:23 (NLT), David says, "But why should I fast when he is dead? Can I bring him back again? I will go to him one day, but he cannot return to me."

I will go to him one day. I will go to Natalie and Noah one day. And for anyone who has lost a baby, you will go to them one day so long as you have faith in Jesus.

As painful as our goodbyes are, they are not finite goodbyes. They are really "see you laters." By faith in Jesus our Lord and Savior, we can see our loved ones again in the heavenly places. This concept resonated so deeply with Jason and me that engraved on Natalie and

Noah's urn is "See you soon." This serves as a reminder to us each day that, before we know it, we will be joyously reunited with them.

Picture a child seeing his or her mother from a distance away and then eagerly running as fast as they can into their mother's open arms. That's what I envision when I think about seeing Natalie and Noah again for the first time. I don't know if it will be anything like that—but it makes me cry every time I think about it. It's a different kind of cry though. It's a hopeful cry. It's a cry of yearning for that day. It's a cry of grief that today isn't that day. And although today isn't that day, I believe it's coming.

Believing this doesn't take away our anguish over our loss, but it can give us hope. And this hope says that even though not a day will go by in this earthly life without us missing those we've lost, by faith in Jesus, not a day will go by in eternity without them with us.

What if you have lost a loved one and you are not sure where their soul lies? What if you don't know if they had faith in Jesus and are in heaven? If that is the case for you, I realize that is a painful unknown to try to reconcile. If this is something you're wrestling through, I want to share some thoughts from Luke 23.

This chapter tells us that when Jesus was crucified, two criminals were led out with him to be crucified as well—one on his right and one on his left (Luke 23:32–33). One of the criminals hurled insults at Jesus, while the other said to Him, "Jesus, remember me when you come into your kingdom" (Luke 23:39, 23:42, NIV). Jesus responds to that man by saying, "Truly I tell you, today you will be with me in paradise" (Luke 23:43, NIV).

A few things stand out to me here:

1) Jesus was there in the final moments of these men's lives; He was *right there* with them—2 Peter 3:9 (NIV) tells us that "he is patient with you, not wanting anyone to perish,

but everyone to come to repentance." Is it possible then that Jesus is there in everyone's last moments?

2) In those last moments, the two criminals each demonstrated a different response to Jesus: the first hurled insults, and the second, despite not having followed Jesus prior to that moment, showed humility and simply asked Jesus to remember him. The second criminal was not necessarily a Christ-follower, but in those moments, he believed that Jesus was about to leave the earth and enter a kingdom demonstrating some level of belief in Him.

3) Jesus responds to the second criminal, "Truly I tell you, today you will be with me in paradise." What if that was Jesus's response to your loved one in their final moments?

I realize that on this side of heaven, there is no way to know for sure what those final moments are like and how each person responds, but consider the what-ifs here. What if your loved one is actually in heaven, having been given one last chance and thereby having received salvation?

While it is true that you don't have any control over how your loved one may have responded, you do have full control over how you respond if you're dealing with a crisis of faith. If you've been reading this book, Jesus is working in you. He is real, and so are heaven and hell. If you're wrestling through things, that's OK and it's normal. But please consider the what-ifs and realize that there *is* hope.

Journal entry from July 8, 2017

Father, this pain and sadness that I'm feeling is unlike anything I've ever experienced. My heart aches for Natalie and Noah … for all the things I had anticipated doing with them and for them. Lord, I'm trying. I'm trying to be strong and to make good decisions, but it's hard and I'm scared. I don't know what the future holds, and that's hard too, but I know that You do and I believe and trust in who You are, that You are for me and with me, and that I am Your daughter. I don't know what's coming, but I know You're going before me. Help me, Father. Please give Natalie and Noah a big hug from their mommy, tell them how much I love them and how happy I am to know that they are with You. Amen.

He will wipe every tear from their eyes, and there will be no more death or sorrow or crying or pain. All these things are gone forever.

—Revelation 21:4 (NLT)

CHAPTER 11

COMMENCE THE CLIMB

The Sovereign Lord is my strength!
He makes me as surefooted as a deer,
able to tread upon the heights.

—Habakkuk 3:19 (NLT)

He makes me as surefooted as a deer,
enabling me to stand on mountain heights.

—Psalm 18:33 (NLT)

In the weeks following Natalie and Noah's deaths, my mom came to our house just about every day to read aloud the book *Hinds' Feet on High Places* to Jason and me. This book, originally written in 1955, is unique because it is written as an allegory. It is the story of a young woman named Much-Afraid who leaves her Fearing family and goes on a journey to the High Places of the Shepherd. She has two companions that guide her along her journey: Sorrow and Suffering. Their journey is filled with many dangers and obstacles, and through it all, we see Much-Afraid growing in maturity as she learns to submit her will to that of the Shepherd while learning to embrace her companions, Sorrow and Suffering. Can you begin to see the relevance of the symbolism here?

The experience of loss results in sorrow and suffering joining us as companions in our life, does it not? They are unwanted and uninvited, but our new companions nonetheless. Living with sorrow and suffering can either break us or bring depth to us. If we let Him, God can use them as tools to shape us, mature our faith, and enable us to endure the devastation of our circumstances—He can use them to bring us to new heights.

Deer that are able to scale remarkably high and dangerous terrain have the specialized ability to place their back feet exactly where their front feet stepped. Apart from this unique capability, they would not be able to reach the heights needed to elude dangerous predators. Similarly, apart from God, we may not be able to reach the heights needed to bear the hardship of our grief.

As both Habakkuk 3:19 and Psalm 18:33 state, God *makes* our feet surefooted; they don't start that way.

The experience of loss can either change us into bitter, angry, faithless people *or* we can allow God to change us through it. God can use sorrow and suffering to make us more like Him. He can use them to teach us about His sovereignty. He can use them to make us more compassionate. He can use them to strengthen our faith. He can use them to deepen our relationship with Him and our relationships with others. He can use them to make us into greater vessels for His use.

The prophet Habakkuk wrote Habakkuk 3 (NLT) after having a vision-like experience from God that indicated destruction was soon coming to Judah because of all the evil happening there. Habakkuk was so burdened by what he had seen of this impending destruction upon his nation that he wrote the following verses (verses 16–19):

> I trembled inside when I heard this;
>   my lips quivered with fear.
> My legs gave way beneath me,
>   and I shook in terror.

> I will wait quietly for the coming day
>> when disaster will strike the people who invade us.
> Even though the fig trees have no blossoms,
>> and there are no grapes on the vines;
> even though the olive crop fails,
>> and the fields lie empty and barren;
> even though the flocks die in the fields,
>> and the cattle barns are empty,
> yet I will rejoice in the Lord!
>> I will be joyful in the God of my salvation!
> The Sovereign Lord is my strength!
> He makes me as surefooted as a deer,
>> able to tread upon the heights.

In the face of the destruction he realized was coming and in the face of overwhelming loss, Habakkuk rejoices in God, professes God as his strength, and proclaims that God *makes* him as surefooted as a deer. He recognizes that it is God who enables him to withstand terrifying circumstances.

On a different note, yet similar tone, David writes Psalm 18 as a song to the Lord after the Lord had rescued him from Saul and his enemies. It is a psalm of praise that followed the suffering, fear, and loss he had endured from Saul and all those against him. He writes verse 33—*He makes me as surefooted as a deer, enabling me to stand on mountain heights*—from a place of experience. This verse is David's testimony of what God brought him through. Some of the preceding verses are as follows:

> I love you, Lord, my strength.
> The Lord is my rock, my fortress and my deliverer;
>> my God is my rock, in whom I take refuge,
>> my shield and the horn of my salvation, my stronghold.

I called to the LORD, who is worthy of praise,
  and I have been saved from my enemies.
The cords of death entangled me;
  the torrents of destruction overwhelmed me.
The cords of the grave coiled around me;
  the snares of death confronted me.
In my distress I called to the LORD;
  I cried to my God for help.
From his temple he heard my voice;
  my cry came before him, into his ears.

He parted the heavens and came down;
  dark clouds were under his feet.
He mounted the cherubim and flew;
  he soared on the wings of the wind.
He made darkness his covering, his canopy
around him—
  the dark rain clouds of the sky.

He reached down from on high and took hold of me;
  he drew me out of deep waters.
He rescued me from my powerful enemy,
  from my foes, who were too strong for me.
They confronted me in the day of my disaster,
  but the LORD was my support.
He brought me out into a spacious place;
  he rescued me because he delighted in me.

—Psalm 18:1–11, 18:16–19 (NIV)

David gives God all the credit here as he communicates that he could not have endured or overcome the challenges he faced apart from God's hand. His painful circumstances led him to encounter God on such an intimate and practical level—one where he experienced God *making* his feet surefooted in the midst of it all.

No one wants to know sorrow and suffering. I wouldn't imagine that Habakkuk and David did. I sure didn't. I'm sure you didn't either. But if we never knew them, we may not be able to reach the same level of heights that God can bring us to through them. If your feet do not feel very sure right now, that's OK. Just believe that He can make them.

Journal entry from July 11, 2017

Heavenly Father, I'm hurting and I miss my babies. My heart breaks that I don't get the chance here on earth to have them and raise them. Father, I know they were a gift from You, and I know that they were Yours ultimately—Yours to give and Yours to take away. God, why is this desire to have children so strong in me? I don't know why, but I have to believe—and I ask and pray—that You would use this desire in my life to bring glory to You, that You would give me strength and wisdom to raise many children from my womb to know You, love You, and serve You. I trust You and I put my hope in You—without that, I don't know how I could continue living with any sort of joy, peace, or purpose. Father, please see me right now and hear me. Father, is this longing for children that I have God-given? And if it is, I just give it to You and ask that You would fulfill it in accordance with Your will. I am believing and trusting that You are working through my loss, pain, and grief to redeem it all. Help me to see it. But until then, and even if I don't, I will look to You and put my hope in You. Father, what good can come from this nightmare in my life? Please use it for Your eternal purposes. Amen.

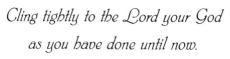

Cling tightly to the Lord your God
as you have done until now.

—Joshua 23:8 (NLT)

CHAPTER 12

NOWHERE ELSE TO GO

There is wonderful joy ahead, even though you must endure
many trials for a little while. These trials will show that your
faith is genuine. It is being tested as fire tests and purifies
gold—though your faith is far more precious than mere gold.
So when your faith remains strong through many trials,
it will bring you much praise and glory and honor on the
day when Jesus Christ is revealed to the whole world.

—1 Peter 1:6–7 (NLT)

During the refining process, gold is heated at extremely high tem-
peratures in order to separate the pure gold from impurities, other
metal contaminants, and dross. The heating process essentially
shows what the gold is really made of, just as the trials we face show
what's really in our hearts.

What do we *really* believe about God?

Who do we *really* believe He is?

Is our faith genuine? Or is it mere religion?

Are our hearts hard and closed off to Him? Or are they soft and
dependent on Him?

As the fire breaks down gold to see what's inside, the tragedies in our lives do the same to us. They break us down to a place where we come face to face with the most pivotal choice we will ever make: to continue walking with God and trusting Him, or not.

Simon Peter's response to Jesus in John 6 (NLT) deeply resonated with me when I was in the midst of facing this choice. In this chapter, Jesus feeds more than five thousand people from five barley loaves and two fish *and* literally walks on water. When crowds of people follow Him the next day, He says to them in verses 26–27, "I tell you the truth, you want to be with me because I fed you, not because you understood the miraculous signs. But don't be so concerned about perishable things like food. Spend your energy seeking the eternal life that the Son of Man can give you."

Jesus is challenging their motives as he recognizes that they are seeking free food from Him rather than spiritual truth. The crowd then goes on to ask Jesus if they also can perform God's works (verse 28), for a miraculous sign (verse 30), and for more bread (verse 34).

Jesus tries to further distinguish between the material and physical things they are seeking and His spiritual teaching in John 6:35–40 when He says, "I am the bread of life. Whoever comes to me will never be hungry again. Whoever believes in me will never be thirsty. But you haven't believed in me even though you have seen me. However, those the Father has given me will come to me, and I will never reject them. For I have come down from heaven to do the will of God who sent me, not to do my own will. And this is the will of God, that I should not lose even one of all those he has given me, but that I should raise them up at the last day. For it is my Father's will that all who see his Son and believe in him should have eternal life. I will raise them up at the last day."

The people then begin to grumble about what He said, argue with each other about what He meant, complain, and question Him. Jesus responds to them further, but their hearts are too hard to believe Him. John 6:66 tells us, "At this point, many of his disciples turned away and deserted him."

These disciples were not deserting Jesus because of experiencing pain and loss in their lives, but the resulting decision they faced is the same one that you and I do—Jesus asks the twelve disciples (verse 67), "Are you also going to leave?"

Simon Peter answers Jesus and says, "Lord, *to whom would we go?* [emphasis mine] You have the words that give eternal life. We believe, and we know you are the Holy One of God" (verses 68–69).

The first time I read this after Natalie and Noah died, it hit me like a ton of bricks. I felt the Lord asking me, "Lindsay, are you also going to leave?"

And I responded to the Lord, saying, "Father, where else would I go? Only You hold my life in the palm of Your hand. Only You hold the lives of my sweet babies. Only You offer salvation to me, though I've done nothing to deserve it or earn it. Only You, Father. So no, Lord, I do not want to leave too. Though my world falls apart around me, I have nowhere else to go but straight into Your arms."

Whether in the face of trying to understand hard spiritual truths as it was for the people in John 6 or in the face of pain and tragedy as it is for us, there are two choices of response to God: to turn your back and walk away or to press in. I can confidently say that I could not have gotten through the pain and heartbreak of losing Natalie and Noah if I had walked away. Choosing to trust God in spite of horrific circumstances doesn't take the pain away, no, and doesn't even alleviate it, but it reveals what's really in our hearts. It shows the authenticity of our faith. It purifies our love for Christ as we learn to love Him for who He is, not for the miracles and physical comforts He can give us.

I doubt that the disciples who deserted Jesus knew the gravity of what they were doing—walking away from the one person who could save them eternally. To *really* believe that Jesus is the Son of God and the Savior of our souls is to know that there is nowhere else to go apart from Him.

Journal entry from July 12, 2017

Heavenly Father, You are my Father, my God, the one and only Almighty Lord, my Protector, my King, my Redeemer, my Savior, my Provider, the One who is worthy of all praise. You are God, and I am not. You are everything, and that is why I fall on my face before You as my life feels to have fallen apart. Where would I go, Lord, apart from You? How could I get through this without You? It's hard enough as it is with You … I profess once again my earnest need for You. I don't know what to do, Lord, other than to seek You. Amen.

*I called on your name, Lord, from deep within the pit.
You heard me when I cried, "Listen to my
pleading! Hear my cry for help!"
Yes, you came when I called; you told me, "Do not fear."*
—Lamentations 3:55–57 (NLT)

CHAPTER 13

NOT AFRAID ANYMORE

God is our refuge and strength,
always ready to help in times of trouble.
So we will not fear when earthquakes come
and the mountains crumble into the sea.

—Psalm 46:1–2 (NLT)

Some people love the thrill of scary movies, but *not* me. I hate watching the scenes when scary music is playing in the background and you just *know* something bad is going to happen. Scary movies are meant to, well, scare you. People who enjoy watching them may find comfort in the fact that they are *just* movies. The scary happening on their television screen is not happening in real life, and when push comes to shove and they get too afraid, they have all power and authority to shut that television off at any moment. But what about when we are afraid in real life? What about when scary *is* happening to us?

During my pregnancy with Natalie and Noah, I ironically struggled with a lot of fear about losing them. I was S-C-A-R-E-D scared. I vividly remember saying to Jason just days before I went into preterm labor, "I don't think I could handle it if anything ever happened to them." Fear is revealing because it shows you where your trust really lies. In my fear, I turned to Psalm 91 (NLT) for comfort. If it has been a while since you've read it, you can read it at the end of this chapter.

I found comfort from verses like verses 3 and 7, which say, "He will rescue you from every trap and protect you from deadly disease" and "though ten thousand are dying around you, these evils will not touch you." I prayed these verses over Natalie and Noah when I was feeling overcome by fear, and I realize now, that I was trusting more in these verses than I was in God Himself.

After Natalie and Noah went to be with Jesus and my fears had come to fruition, I had some major questions for God about these verses in Psalms:

God, how could You let this happen when I prayed this Psalm of protection over them?

God, what's even the point of Psalm 91 if what it says isn't always true?

God, why did You let me find such comfort from this if I was in fact going to lose them?

In the midst of my questioning, God began to show me the true significance of Psalm 91. He revealed to me that it is not meant to be a "name it and claim it" promise of supernatural protection from anything and everything in this life. God certainly can intervene in situations to protect us and our loved ones from harm, and He does at times, but not always. My focus had been wrong. I was focusing on the protection statements—trusting in *them*—when I should have been focusing on what the Psalm says about who God is to us during trouble—trusting in *Him*.

He is our shelter and our rest (verse 1).

He is our refuge and place of safety (verse 2).

His faithful promises are our armor and protection (verse 4).

He will be with us in trouble (verse 15).

Psalm 91 is not a promise of absolute protection, but rather an assurance that if we remain in God, the tragedies we face will not prevail over us. And for that reason, we do not need to live in fear.

Losing Natalie and Noah was, in my eyes, the worst and scariest thing that could have happened to me—it still is actually. I truly did not know if I could handle it, but each day following their loss, God sustained me. He alone is the reason why I survived it, and I came to realize that if He sustained me through that, He can sustain me through anything.

Living through my worst fear taught me not to fear—as oxymoronic as that sounds. I had faced my earthquakes, my mountains had crumbled into the sea, and God was with me through it all.

We see this truth reinforced—this very hard lesson that I learned—all throughout the Bible. David writes in Psalm 34:4 (NIV), "I sought the Lord, and he answered me; he delivered me from all my fears."

Again, in Psalm 56:3 (NIV), David writes, "When I am afraid, I put my trust in you."

It stands out to me that David does not write, "When I am afraid, I trust in God's promise of protection" or "When I am afraid, I trust that nothing bad will happen." He says, "When I am afraid, I trust in *you* [God]." David does not proclaim trust in circumstances or in the maintenance of his well-being; rather, He proclaims trust in God alone.

God Himself also speaks to us through the prophet Isaiah in Isaiah 41:10 (NIV):

> So do not fear, for I am with you; do not be dismayed, for I am your God. I will strengthen you and help you; I will uphold you with my righteous right hand.

The Message version says it this way:

> Don't panic. I'm with you. There's no need to fear
> for I'm your God. I'll give you strength. I'll help
> you. I'll hold you steady, keep a firm grip on you.

God is communicating here His sufficiency. He alone is enough. He alone is all we need. Of course we can ask Him for protection and of course He intercedes for us in accordance with His will, but even when He doesn't, it's not that He has forgotten us, turned away for a moment, or our prayers have slipped through the cracks. No, He is with us *always*, even when prayers go unanswered, even when pain touches our lives, even when the worst possible has happened. Jesus says in Matthew 28:20 (NLT), "And be sure of this: I am with you always, even to the end of the age."

When I was scared about losing Natalie and Noah, *He was with me.*

When I did actually lose them, *He was with me.*

As I continue to grieve over their loss, *He is with me.*

When all is well and when all is not, He is with me—just as He is now with you.

> Those who live in the shelter of the Most High
>   will find rest in the shadow of the Almighty.
> This I declare about the Lord:
> He alone is my refuge, my place of safety;
>   he is my God, and I trust him.
> For he will rescue you from every trap
>   and protect you from deadly disease.
> He will cover you with his feathers.
>   He will shelter you with his wings.
>   His faithful promises are your armor and protection.
> Do not be afraid of the terrors of the night,
>   nor the arrow that flies in the day.

Do not dread the disease that stalks in darkness,
  nor the disaster that strikes at midday.
Though a thousand fall at your side,
  though ten thousand are dying around you,
  these evils will not touch you.
Just open your eyes,
  and see how the wicked are punished.
If you make the Lord your refuge,
  if you make the Most High your shelter,
no evil will conquer you;
  no plague will come near your home.
For he will order his angels
  to protect you wherever you go.
They will hold you up with their hands
  so you won't even hurt your foot on a stone.
You will trample upon lions and cobras;
  you will crush fierce lions and serpents under your feet!
The Lord says, "I will rescue those who love me.
  I will protect those who trust in my name.
When they call on me, I will answer;
  I will be with them in trouble.
  I will rescue and honor them.
I will reward them with a long life
  and give them my salvation. (Psalm 91, NLT)

Heavenly Father, I profess that You are my refuge and my strength. It feels like earthquakes have come and mountains are crumbling around me, and I'm trying not to fear but it's hard. Father, the pain I feel is so deep. I feel like there are two pieces of me missing. Lord, help me to see Your purposes for this in my life. As I sit here in Natalie and Noah's room, I humbly ask, Lord, that You would fill it with laughter again instead of all my tears. I profess that You are good and faithful even when everything around me doesn't seem good. You never change, and You hold my life in the palm of Your hand. Help me, Lord, not to be afraid anymore as I hold tightly to You. Amen.

Now stand here and see the great thing
the Lord is about to do!

—1 Samuel 12:16 (NLT)

CHAPTER 14

Under Construction

> God, pick up the pieces.
> Put me back together again.
> You are my praise!
>
> —Jeremiah 17:14 (MSG)

I love watching the creativity of my four-year-old daughter when she builds things with her mega-blocks—how she very meticulously chooses each block that has the particular color and shape she's looking for and places them in a precise way to create something exciting, entirely unique, and quite special. Her building creations are masterpieces representing her vision for what she was hoping to create.

The only problem with her specially built creations is that they typically don't stand the chance of surviving the advances of her two-year-old brother, who is often in the vicinity. As hard as I may try to keep him away and occupied by other things, that little sneaky boy almost always finds a way to knock down what she has built.

And when that happens, it is *not* a happy time for my daughter as her handcrafted vision is destroyed in the blink of an eye. When

I try to console her and encourage her to start rebuilding it, she is often too despondent and discouraged to even want to try.

So Mama steps in. I don't say, "Sorry, honey, better luck next time" or "That's too bad. Maybe try again tomorrow." I sit down on the floor with her, and I help her. I help her try to remember which blocks go where and the particular structure and color array of the original masterpiece until we get it just right. It normally doesn't look exactly like it did the first time, but with my help, it *is* rebuilt.

Losing a baby is like this in ways. When we're expecting, we build for ourselves an entire vision of what our lives are going to look like with that baby, who will grow into a child, who will grow into a teenager, who will grow into an adult, and so on. We dream, plan, hope, and envision all with such excitement, anticipation, and desire.

And then, in an instant, it's all gone. Loss leaves us entirely disoriented as all our expectations for our future and the vision that we've built are knocked down.

Destroyed.

Crushed.

Broken to pieces.

It's hard to imagine in the midst of it how our lives could ever be put back together again. Just as it is for my four-year-old daughter who is too overcome by disheartenment to rebuild what's been broken without Mama's help, left on our own we can't either.

But we have a God who knows exactly how to step into our brokenness and help us begin to pick up the pieces. We have a God who sees our despondency, sits down on the floor with us, and helps us rebuild what seems to us unbuildable.

Let's look at how this concept is illustrated in the following passage from Ezekiel 37:1–10 (NLT). Ezekiel writes:

> The Lord took hold of me, and I was carried away by the Spirit of the Lord to a valley filled with bones. He led me all around among the bones that covered the valley floor. They were scattered everywhere

across the ground and were completely dried out. Then he asked me, "Son of man, can these bones become living people again?"

"O Sovereign Lord," I replied, "you alone know the answer to that."

Then he said to me, "Speak a prophetic message to these bones and say, 'Dry bones, listen to the word of the Lord! This is what the Sovereign Lord says: Look! I am going to put breath into you and make you live again! I will put flesh and muscles on you and cover you with skin. I will put breath into you, and you will come to life. Then you will know that I am the Lord.'"

So I spoke this message, just as he told me. Suddenly as I spoke, there was a rattling noise all across the valley. The bones of each body came together and attached themselves as complete skeletons. Then as I watched, muscles and flesh formed over the bones. Then skin formed to cover their bodies, but they still had no breath in them.

Then he said to me, "Speak a prophetic message to the winds, son of man. Speak a prophetic message and say, 'This is what the Sovereign Lord says: Come, O breath, from the four winds! Breathe into these dead bodies so they may live again.'"

So I spoke the message as he commanded me, and breath came into their bodies. They all came to life and stood up on their feet—a great army."

In this passage, we see God accomplishing what *only* He can accomplish—not just the unlikely, but the impossible. The bones that God brought back to life, that He formed into a great army, are described as being scattered everywhere across the ground and completely dried out. It was not full skeletons that covered the valley floor, but rather singular pieces of *dry* bones. For the bones to have been completely dried out means that they must have been lying around in that valley for quite a while. One could argue that there could be *some* life left in the bones of the deceased, but certainly not in dried-up, fragmented bones. The thought of a mass of skeletons being brought to life sounds impossible enough—but a valley of dry bone pieces? God must be trying to make a point here.

If God can take a valley of dry bones and form them into a living army, He can take the broken pieces of our lives and put them back together too. He can help us rebuild all that's been knocked down. He can breathe life back into our lives, our vision, and into *us*. Our lives will never be the same as they were before our loss, no, just as the same is true for my daughter's building masterpieces when they are broken down. But when God steps into our desperate situations just as I do for my daughter, He can bring healing to us in ways that are not possible apart from Him.

In Ezekiel 37:11–14 (NLT), which follows the passage we just read, God reveals that the vision He gave to Ezekiel is meant to illustrate His promised revival and restoration of the house of Israel. Verse 11 says,

> Then He [God] said to me, "Son of man, these bones represent the people of Israel. They are saying, 'We have become old, dry bones—*all hope is gone* [emphasis mine]. Our nation is finished.'"

The only hope for the house of Israel's restoration from the desolation caused by their rebellion and sin is God. In the same way, the only lasting hope for you and me for restoration from the desolation caused by our loss is God. Only He can pick up our broken pieces and help us put them back together.

I can't tell you exactly what that will look like for your life, but I can tell you that as I laid my broken pieces before Him all those years ago, He was so gracious and faithful in picking each one up for me. My pain remains a part of me and I still live with some extent of brokenness, but He *did* put my life back together. He put me back together. Some of my pieces are still cracked and scarred, but that's OK—I don't think those pieces will be fully healed until this earthly life has passed and I stand in the presence of Jesus. So I like to think of myself now as wholly broken before Him—having experienced Him putting my life back together when my life was in pieces. I've been broken, yes, but I've also been made whole by Him and in Him.

May you too lay your broken pieces before Him today, and see what He will do.

Journal entry from July 16, 2017

Heavenly Father, I can't believe it has been one whole month since Natalie's birth and death. Tomorrow will be one month since Noah's birth and death. Father, as my hopes and desires for my future and what's to come have been shattered, I look up to You. I bring all those broken pieces before You and lay them at Your feet. I recognize that I have very little (no) control over what's to come, so, Father, please, may Your will be done in my life. Please put all these broken pieces back together. Please teach me what You need to from this loss. God, You know my heart and everything about me. All I can do is trust my heart to You and trust my life to You. Lord, would You make rivers in the dry wasteland of my life and part the seas ahead of me? For on my own, I am lost, and on my own, I can do nothing and have nothing. And I don't want anything in this life that's not from Your hand. Amen.

Abraham believed in the God who brings the dead back to life and who creates new things out of nothing. Even when there was no reason for hope, Abraham kept hoping.

—Romans 4:17–18 (NLT)

CHAPTER 15

Hope That Never Disappoints

Jesus Christ is the same yesterday, today, and forever.

—Hebrews 13:8 (NLT)

We put our hope in the Lord. He is our help and our shield.
In him our hearts rejoice, for we trust in his holy name.
Let your unfailing love surround us, Lord,
for our hope is in you alone.

—Psalm 33:20–22 (NLT)

One of the most important lessons I learned from losing Natalie and Noah is that so much in this earthly life is temporary, unreliable, and fading. I learned that hope in anything apart from Christ is futile and sets us up for disappointment. Our lives can change in an instant, as we who have lost loved ones well know. Changes are often unexpected and unwanted. The only thing that we can rely on to be eternally unchanging is God.

A ship's anchor enables it to remain in one place by combating the ever-changing currents and winds that otherwise would drag the ship off course. Similarly, hope in God serves as the anchor in our ever-changing worlds. Hebrews 6:18–19 (NLT) tells us,

> Therefore, we who have fled to him for refuge can have great confidence as we hold to the hope that lies before us. This hope is a strong and trustworthy anchor for our souls.

Hope in God provides the only source of true, dependable stability for our lives. Placing our hope in outcomes is so dangerous because outcomes are always unpredictable and are often out of our control.

During my pregnancy with Natalie and Noah, I admit that my hope was probably placed more in them being born and coming home with me than in God and His sovereignty. I entirely expected them to be born safely and to live life with them. I was ignorant in a lot of ways. I shared previously that I struggled with fear of something bad happening to them during my pregnancy. But even with that fear, I don't think I really believed that something bad would happen, so much so that when I started going into preterm labor, I had no concept of the gravity of what was happening. Even as Jason and I left our house to go to the hospital, we talked about stopping somewhere to get breakfast afterward before heading to work. My expectation for pregnancy was that it would result in taking home a baby, and I realize now that my hope was largely placed in that expected outcome.

Since their loss, I hold on to my hopes for my life very lightly. Instead, I hold on to my only finite hope, Jesus, for dear life.

Of course, we will always have hope for things, and that's completely normal and fine. We will always hope for such and such to happen or not happen—but we shouldn't hope *in* those things or place our confidence in them. Regarding this, the apostle James writes in James 4:13–16 (NLT),

> Look here, you who say, "Today or tomorrow we are going to a certain town and will stay there a year. We will do business there and make a profit." How do you know what your life will be like tomorrow? Your life is like the morning fog—it's here a little while, then it's gone. What you ought to say is, "If the Lord wants us to, we will live and do this or that." Otherwise, you are boasting about your own pretentious plans …

I don't know about you, but that challenges me. To live a life wholly submitted to the will of God is to place our confidence and reliance on Him alone and to know Him as our firm foundation that never changes or casts a shifting shadow even in all the unknowns of our tomorrows.

We hope *in* Him alone because our hopes *for* anything else are so unreliable—and that is something He will never be. Hebrews 10:23 (NIV) exhorts us, "Let us hold unswervingly to the hope we profess, for he who promised is faithful."

Other translations use phrases including *hold fast, hold tightly*, and *hold firmly*. If you're holding on to something with that much intention, vigor, steadfastness, and resolve, you won't be reaching out, trying to hold on to other things that might unsteady you. In the same way, as we hold unswervingly, fast, tightly, and firmly to our hope in God, the same is true for us.

This has been a hard lesson for me to learn. But it was one I needed to learn, and it is one that has since then carried me through day-to-day disappointments and ambiguity. I try with intention now to hold loosely to things of this life and, rather, hold firmly to my confident hope in Jesus. Will you do the same?

Journal entry from July 19, 2017

Father, I yearn for You and I cling to You. I seek You this morning with all my heart for I am in desperate need of You. I recognize that I have simply no control over so much and that You are Almighty God, my sovereign Lord, the Creator of all the universe. So humbly I come before You. Please reveal Yourself to me, show me which paths to take, please heal my heart, please give me grace and strength, and please keep me in the center of Your will. Father, as I reflect on my life and the things You have brought me through, I so clearly see Your faithfulness, grace, and provision. You have been so faithful and good to me. And You are the same yesterday, today, and tomorrow. You are faithful and good now, even as my life in my eyes just seems to crumble before me and as my heart is breaking. Even as everything has changed, You have not changed. So this morning, Father, I hold firmly to Your faithfulness. The only thing I can fully rely on in this life is You. Father, see my heart—my heart is Yours. Amen.

Lessons I am learning after losing Natalie and Noah:

- *the importance of living day by day, taking each day as it comes and not thinking too far ahead,*
- *my hope needs to be in God and who He is, not in outcomes,*
- *God will meet me where I am; even when it seems like He must have left or is absent, He is always right here and He never leaves me, and*
- *everything in this life is temporary and fading— my eyes need to be fixed on eternal things.*

CHAPTER 16

Don't Stop Now

Come, let us return to the Lord. He has torn us to pieces;
now he will heal us. He has injured us; now he will bandage
our wounds. In just a short time he will restore us, so that we
may live in his presence. Oh, that we might know the Lord!
Let us press on to know him. He will respond to us as surely
as the arrival of dawn or the coming of rains in early spring.

—Hosea 6:1–3 (NLT)

We live in a world obsessed with instant gratification, quick fixes,
easy, and fast. Have something that's not working for you? Throw
it out and buy a new one. Can't find the television remote? Amazon
could probably have one delivered to you the next day. Latest fad not
making you as satisfied as you thought it would? Forget it and move
on to the next one. Is Christianity not meeting your expectations
for happiness? Well, who needs Jesus anyway? I'm, of course, being
facetious with that last one, but I think you get my point.

In a world that says, "If it's not working, try something else," how
do we respond when God hasn't shown up for us like we expected
Him to? When the worst has happened and He didn't stop it?

The prophet Hosea has an important word for us today regarding this: let us *press on* to know Him. If ever we needed to hear this, it's now. The phrase "press on" implies that there is some kind of obstacle either in your way or that could hold you back from moving toward whatever the goal is. It implies that you're facing something hard and that getting through it may require some work and effort on your part.

For the Israelites at the time Hosea 6:1–3 was written, their obstacle was their continual rebellion against God, which resulted in His judgment upon them. In the face of the consequences of their sin, it was not the time for flippancy or passiveness. They needed to take action. They needed to return to Him, repent, and press on in their relationship with Him. If they didn't, their sin and the resulting judgment they were facing would prevent them from right standing with God and from receiving all He had in store for them.

For me and you, our obstacle is obvious: we have suffered unimaginable loss. This obstacle could either hold us back from our walks with Christ *or* be a catalyst that deepens our walk with Him. The determining factor to which is entirely dependent on our response. In order for it to be the latter, we need to *press on* toward Him despite our circumstances, questions, and pain.

How can this be done practically? By seeking Him every day. By making Him a priority in your life. By investing your time and energy in things that will draw you closer to Him. Read the Bible, pray, listen to worship music—do anything you can to consume yourself with Him each day. Even when you don't feel like it, press on toward Him anyway. Your flesh may not *want* to, I know, but I promise you will not regret it.

The prophet Hosea assures the Israelites in Hosea 6:1–3 that if they do their part, God will respond to them as surely as the arrival of dawn or the coming of rains in early spring. I believe the same holds true for us. Psalm 102:17 (NLT) says,

> He will listen to the prayers of the destitute. He will
> not reject their pleas.

David writes in Psalm 3:4 (NLT),

> I cried out to the Lord, and he answered me from his holy mountain.

And Jesus Himself says in Luke 11:9–13 (NLT),

> And so I tell you, keep on asking, and you will receive what you ask for. Keep on seeking, and you will find. Keep on knocking, and the door will be opened to you. For everyone who asks, receives. Everyone who seeks, finds. And to everyone who knocks, the door will be opened.
>
> You fathers—if your children ask for a fish, do you give them a snake instead? Or if they ask for an egg, do you give them a scorpion? Of course not! So if you sinful people know how to give good gifts to your children, how much more will your heavenly Father give the Holy Spirit to those who ask him.

Notice how in all three of these scripture references, God's response follows the actions of *praying* and *pleading* in Psalm 102, *crying out* in Psalm 3, and *asking, seeking,* and *knocking* in Luke 11. This is what pressing on looks like. And how exactly does God respond in these examples? By *listening* and *accepting* in Psalm 102, *answering* in Psalm 3, and *giving, revealing,* and *working* in Luke 11. This is what our God does.

In the aftermath of my loss of Natalie and Noah, I can testify to God's response to my pursuit of Him. As I sought Him each day, He never failed to show up for me. Every time I read back through my prayer journal from that time period, I am reminded of that and awed by God's graciousness to me.

I wasn't left to deal with my grief alone, He was with me.

I wasn't chastised for my questions, He showed me compassion.

I wasn't crying out to a faraway, apathetic God; He answered me, revealed Himself to me, provided for me, and taught me.

Pressing on toward Him despite my grief has enabled me to know Him deeper and greater than I ever could have otherwise. In the midst of the mess of my life, He met me every time with open arms as my loving Father.

In a world that says, "If it's not working, try something else," God is not something to be thrown out, replaced, moved on from, or glossed over. If He hasn't been "working" for you like you hoped, then it may be your perspective that needs to be replaced or rejected, not Him. In a world that is inherently broken, He's not; and in a life that is in shambles, He is our greatest need, not because of what He can do for us, but because of what He already has done for us in the life, death, and resurrection of Jesus Christ. So as Hosea wrote to the Israelites in Hosea 6:3 (NLT), I write to you:

> Oh, that we might know the Lord! Let us press on to know him. He will respond to us as surely as the arrival of dawn or the coming of rains in early spring.

Journal entry from July 21, 2017

Heavenly Father, I look to You and You alone this morning. I empty myself before You. I empty my pain, fears, sorrow, grief, disappointments, worries, and anger. I empty all of it before You and ask that You would fill me now with Yourself, Your truth, Your word, and Your love. I press into You, Father. What do You want from me now? What do I do? Please help me to see that I have a future and a hope. Father, may this Valley of Weeping I'm lying in become a place of refreshing springs. May the autumn rains clothe this valley with blessings. Lord, I'm feeling exhausted, like every step in every day is weighted with grief and confusion. I'm tired, Father, so please sustain me as I lean hard on You. Please give Natalie and Noah a hug and a kiss from their mommy and tell them that I miss them deeply. Amen.

The Lord is close to the brokenhearted;
he rescues those whose spirits are crushed.
The righteous person faces many troubles,
but the Lord comes to the rescue each time.

—Psalm 34:18–19 (NLT)

CHAPTER 17

THE BATTLE BEFORE ME

For we have no power against this great
multitude that is coming against us;
nor do we do not know what to do,
but our eyes are upon You.

—2 Chronicles 20:12 (NKJV)

In 2 Chronicles 20 (NKJV), Jehoshaphat is told that "a great multitude is coming against [him] from beyond the sea, from Syria" (verse 2). This multitude included the people of Moab, the people of Ammon, and others besides the Ammonites, and they came to battle against Jehoshaphat and his kingdom. Verses 3–4 tell us that after learning about this vast army approaching,

> Jehoshaphat feared, and set himself to seek the Lord, and proclaimed a fast throughout all Judah. So Judah gathered together to ask help from the Lord; and from all the cities of Judah they came to seek the Lord.

Jehoshaphat then leads this assembly of people in prayer as he cries out to God for help, wisdom, and direction. He begins his prayer with the recognition of God's power, sovereignty, and the great works He has performed in years past:

> O Lord God of our fathers, are You not God in heaven, and do You not rule over all the kingdoms of the nations, and in Your hand is there not power and might, so that no one is able to withstand You? Are You not our God, who drove out the inhabitants of this land before Your people Israel, and gave it to the descendants of Abraham Your friend forever? (2 Chronicles 20:6–7)

The end of Jehoshaphat's prayer is what I especially want to highlight as he humbles himself before God and demonstrates authentic trust in Him in the midst of terrifying circumstances:

> Our God, will You not judge them? For we have no power against this great multitude that is coming against us; nor do we do not know what to do, but our eyes are upon You. (2 Chronicles 20:12)

We do not know what to do, but our eyes are on you. This strongly resonated with me after losing Natalie and Noah, and it continues to. Like Jehoshaphat, I had no idea what to do. It felt like a vast army had just devastated my life and I didn't know how I was going to survive it. I was so terrified by what was before me: life without Natalie and Noah. I was desperate for help, hope, and direction, so day after day, I cried out to the only One whom I knew could provide me with those things.

When it feels as though we are facing a vast army, we must set our eyes on God rather than the devastation before us. The only place where enduring help will come from is through Him.

In 2 Chronicles 20:15, God responds to Jehoshaphat's prayer and says,

> Do not be afraid nor dismayed because of this great multitude, for the battle is not yours, but God's.

I believe that God wants to speak this to you today as well.

During my quiet time with God following my losses, He showed up every time to help me fight my battle. He gave me what I needed for each terrifying day that was before me. The fight still wasn't easy, but He made it possible. I often wonder how it is that anyone makes it through the tragedies of this life without the hope and help that we have in Jesus. I don't think I would have. It is hard enough as it is walking through it *with* Him.

For Jehoshaphat, he still had to go out and face the vast army that was against him. In 2 Chronicles 20:16–17, God says,

> Tomorrow go down against them. They will surely come up by the Ascent of Ziz, and you will find them at the end of the brook before the Wilderness of Jeruel. You will not need to fight in this battle. Position yourselves, stand still and see the salvation of the Lord, who is with you, O Judah and Jerusalem!

Jehoshaphat had to go down against them and believe that God was going to come to his rescue. He had to believe that everything God said was true, that God was able, and that God would be with him. And we need to believe all those things as well.

If we look at the end of the story here in 2 Chronicles 20:22, we learn the outcome:

> When they began to sing and to praise, the Lord set ambushes against the people of Ammon, Moab,

and Mount Seir, who had come against Judah; and
they were defeated.

God always keeps His word. As He defeated the army before
Jehoshaphat, He can defeat the one standing before you as well.

If you're feeling anything like Jehoshaphat was in 2 Chronicles
(*"for we have no power to face this vast army that is attacking us"*),
take heart and follow Jehoshaphat's example: *"We do not know what
to do, but our eyes are on you."*

Heavenly Father, I have set my heart on You. You have every part of me. This has been a hard lesson to learn, Lord—that no matter what this life brings or what is taken away, You are the only constant thing I can depend on. I don't know what to do now, Father, so all I can do is look to You. Thank You that Your faithfulness, goodness, and grace never waver. Thank You for this life You've given me and for Your provision of Natalie and Noah. Thank You that I got to carry them for as long as I did. Thank You that I got to see their faces and hold them. Thank You that they are with You and that I will see them again. Thank You for the family in heaven You've given me. Now, Lord, would You lead me in each day forward? Would You give me the strength to keep living fully and for Your glory? Father, You know my heart and my heart's desires, so I lay them at Your feet and trust them to You. I fix my eyes on You today. Amen.

Some wandered in the wilderness,
lost and homeless.
Hungry and thirsty,
they nearly died.
"Lord, help!" they cried in their trouble,
and he rescued them from their distress.
He led them straight to safety,
to a city where they could live.
Let them praise the Lord for his great love
and for the wonderful things he has done for them.
For he satisfies the thirsty
and fills the hungry with good things.

—Psalm 107:4–9 (NLT)

CHAPTER 18

GOING NORTH

We wandered around in the region of Mount Seir for a long time.
Then at last the Lord said to me, "You have been wandering
around in this hill country long enough; turn to the north."

—Deuteronomy 2:1–3 (NLT)

In the days and weeks following my losses, it was hard to do *anything*.
If it weren't for my mom coming over every day and putting food in
front of me, I don't think I would have eaten. I barely got out of my
pajamas, didn't watch television, and didn't clean my house. If I'm
being honest, I felt like becoming a bitter recluse of a woman who
confined herself to her dark basement. That way, I could just sit and
dwell in my grief without any responsibilities otherwise.

After days of living (or not living) like this, I remember my mom
encouraging Jason and me to go outside for a walk. I did *not* want
to but decided to appease my mom by saying I would go just to the
end of the road, which was not far. Well, when Jason and I got to
the end of the road, I realized that it actually felt OK to be walking,
and it seemed to be providing an opportunity for us to actually talk
and begin processing our grief. From that day on, walking became a
big part of our grief process. Jason began looking up different places

to walk in wooded areas where there wouldn't be a lot of people around, and we would go to these places and just walk. We would literally go and wander.

On one of these walks, we stumbled upon a large hornet's nest that appeared to be vacant hanging from the branch of a tree. Jason, being Jason, decided it was a good idea to throw a rock at the hornet's nest. Just as he released the rock toward the nest, an angry hornet flew out of the nest and hit him right in the middle of the forehead. As the rock then hit the nest, unleashing a full swarm of angry hornets in our direction, he yelled at me, "Run!" Which we did as you can imagine. Note to self: one should not be running from angry hornets in the forest just weeks after giving birth twice. Note to Jason: just because a hornet's nest appears vacant doesn't mean that it is. I think that may be the only instance from that time period that we can look back on and laugh.

We also stumbled upon other things during our walks: a pond filled with frogs, a steep embankment we carefully slid down, sometimes animals, sometimes nothing interesting at all. But as we wandered, we processed. We reflected. We talked about Natalie and Noah. We talked about our pain. We talked about our life thereafter. I would highly recommend walking as a process tool in your grief.

But going to different places to walk and wander every day meant that there were a lot of things in my life I *wasn't* doing and a lot of places I *wasn't* going. That is exactly what "wandering" implies—that you're not moving toward any kind of destination. While I wandered, I was entirely disengaged from the rest of my life. I think that this was absolutely necessary for the time being as it enabled me to grieve more productively and purposely.

Deuteronomy 2 tells us that the Israelites wandered for a time too, though for a very different reason: they wandered in the wilderness as a punishment for their disobedience to God. Despite this vast difference in why they wandered, I believe that the message God gave to them in Deuteronomy 2:3 is similar to the one He at some point wants to give to us:

> You have been wandering around in this hill country
> long enough; turn to the north.

To the Israelites, this meant that it was time to leave the hill country they had been wandering in and begin literally walking north toward the land that God had promised to give them. God was instructing them to begin walking in the direction of His will for their lives. To us, this might mean that it's time to start reengaging with the lives He's calling us to. For me, this looked like going back to work, going back to church, and beginning to spend time with friends and family again—to stop spending each day literally wandering in the woods, and start living again.

At that point in time, I felt God calling me to

Turn to the north. Begin walking again toward a life lived surrendered to Him.

Turn to the north. Begin living again in remembrance of Natalie and Noah.

Turn to the north. Begin living each day in a way that honors Natalie and Noah and would make them proud.

Turn to the north. Begin living out my belief that He has plans to use this in my life and recognize that He can't accomplish them if I remain wandering in the wilderness.

If the Israelites remained wandering in the hill country, never turning north, they would not have been able to reach the destination God wanted to lead them to or fulfill the purposes He had for them. The same holds true for me and you.

This by *no means whatsoever* means that we should just move on with our lives. I realize that I stated this already, but it's worth emphasizing again: we will *never* move on, but at some point, we are called to move forward. Moving on and moving forward are two very different things.

Moving on implies getting over something, forgetting about it, and leaving it behind. That will never be true for us. Similarly, when God instructed the Israelites to turn to the north, He wasn't asking them to move on either. In the book of Deuteronomy, the verb "remember" (Hebrew *zachor*) is used more than a dozen times. Deuteronomy is essentially a book of remembrance. Throughout it, Moses is continually calling the Israelites to remember all that had happened to them up to that point, to remember all that God had done for them, to remember everything He said, everything He provided, and everything He revealed to them.

In Deuteronomy 4:9 (NIV), Moses tells them, "Only be careful and watch yourselves closely so that you do not forget the things your eyes have seen or let them fade from your heart as long as you live."

Their call was not to move on from the hardships they had faced, pretending they never happened or to live unchanged by them, but rather to *always* remember and move forward.

I believe this is the same call for you and me. When exactly this call comes will likely be different for everyone. I think that a time of wandering, however that may look, is a necessary part of the grieving process and there is no time constraint on it. It may be weeks, it may be months, but however long, there will come a point when God begins whispering to your heart, "Turn to the north, remember, and move forward."

When I began turning to the north, I was an absolute wreck doing so, but I was obedient to what I felt God calling me to. In the first many weeks back to work and church, I cried … a lot. When I began spending time with friends and family again, it was hard to be present with them and to smile or laugh. But as I continued to go through the motions, I eventually figured out that I could continue walking in the will of God for my life by doing what He put in front of me each day *while* carrying Natalie and Noah in my heart and mind in remembrance.

As I've turned to the north and continued to walk in God's will for my life, I've been able to share and live out Natalie and Noah's story. If I had stayed wandering in the forest, that would not have happened. Truly, their memory and significance can best live on through my life lived in God's will. And on that blessed day when I stand before my Savior and see my babies again, I hope to be able to say to them both, "I tried my best to live well for you."

It's more than OK to wander for however long you need, but as you do, listen for whenever the call of God comes to *turn to the north.*

Journal entry from July 27, 2017

Father, I feel like a scared little child who doesn't know her way around. Please give me an understanding heart and wisdom from You so that I may find life through You and walk in Your ways and Your will always. Father, I seek You for direction and for what I need to move forward in Your will. I profess my need for You and that on my own, I can do nothing. Anything I do is by Your strength and grace, and everything I have is from Your hand. Lord, I miss Natalie and Noah. It's still hard to think about living without them, so please help me find a way to live well for them and for You. Amen.

But I trust in the Lord [and rely on
Him with unwavering confidence].
I will rejoice and be glad in Your steadfast love,
Because You have seen my affliction;
You have taken note of my life's distresses.

—Psalm 31:6–7 (Amplified Bible)

CHAPTER 19

REALITY CHECK

Sorrowful, yet always rejoicing;
poor, yet making many rich;
having nothing, and yet possessing everything.

—2 Corinthians 6:10 (NIV)

While I was pregnant with Natalie and Noah, one of my best friends at the time was pregnant too, with our due dates about one month apart. It was so exciting being pregnant together! Jason and I went with her and her husband on a "babymoon" about halfway through our pregnancies. We rented a condo on the beach in Myrtle Beach, SC, and spent a week enjoying our last anticipated baby-less vacation. I have such happy memories of that week. We took lots of pictures of our bellies, which had grown quite big by then, and shopped for nursery décor—it was fabulous.

After Natalie and Noah died, our friendship inevitably changed. I didn't want it to, but our circumstances made it unavoidable. The reality was that she was still pregnant, and I was not. As much as I didn't intend for or want it to pain me to see her progressively growing belly, it did.

As we deal with the aftermath of our losses, it is really OK to take a step back from relationships and circumstances that are intensely triggering. It may be just for a time, or maybe for a long time, but it's important for us to give ourselves permission to do so and for those around us to understand that it has nothing to do inherently with them and is no one's fault—rather, it is just an unfortunate consequence. For me, this meant I did have to take a step back from my friendship with my friend. I was still excited for her, yes. But I was at the same time profoundly anguished for myself.

When she gave birth to her son right around the time I would have been giving birth to Natalie and Noah had they been full-term, I was genuinely happy for her, *and* I was full of sorrow.

When I went to see her and her newborn baby for the first time, I rejoiced with her, *and* I grieved deeply that Natalie and Noah weren't here.

It was simply impossible for me to joyfully look at her son without mournfully thinking of Natalie and Noah.

After loss, it seems that simultaneous and contradictory emotions become an everyday part of our lives. We can feel emotions at the same exact moment that feel so opposing to one another, and yet we can feel both so strongly. Now, six years later, that reality still holds true. Pain and sadness have become everyday parts of my life because the pain and sadness from loss do not just go away—I don't think they ever do. I will *always* wish Natalie and Noah were here with me. I will *never* be OK with what happened. But I have learned that pain and sadness can live simultaneously with joy and peace in Christ.

- We can want our babies or those we've lost back every day *and* we can be grateful for those who are still here with us.
- We can miss them with all of our heart *and* we can love God with all of our heart.
- We can wish they were here with us *and* still live a life that makes them proud.
- We can yearn for the day when we'll be with them again in the heavenly places *and* we can yearn every day for more of Jesus.

- We can feel angry about what happened *and* we can submit to God's sovereignty.
- We can lack understanding of the whys *and* we can rest knowing that He holds all understanding.
- We can cry *and* we can praise.
- We can mourn *and* we can trust.
- We can feel pain that is unbearable *and* feel the comfort of His presence.
- We can be broken *and* be a vessel of use for His kingdom.
- We can live each day changed by our loss *and* we can live each day changed by God through it.
- We can lie weeping and dejected *and* we can find hope in God.

You see, our lives after loss become filled with the coexistence of seemingly contrasting thoughts, feelings, and actions. But as contradictory as they seem, they actually aren't; they go together, hand in hand as we stand hand in hand with Jesus.

In 2 Corinthians 4:8–9 (NLT), the apostle Paul puts it this way:

> We are pressed on every side by troubles, but we are not crushed. We are perplexed, but not driven to despair. We are hunted down, but never abandoned by God. We get knocked down, but we are not destroyed.

And as we read at the beginning of the chapter in 2 Corinthians 6:10 (NIV), also written by the apostle Paul,

> Sorrowful, yet always rejoicing; poor, yet making many rich; having nothing, and yet possessing everything.

Having nothing, and yet possessing everything. Let that soak in for a minute—that we can simultaneously have nothing *and* possess everything so long as we have Jesus.

Loss can change things for the worse, yes—our circumstances, realities, relationships, and well-being. But when God changes *us*, so can our perspective to where we can view all these derivative losses through the lens of *having nothing, and yet possessing everything.* The apostle Paul encourages us in 2 Corinthians 4:6–7 (NLT),

> For God, who said, "Let there be light in the darkness," has made this light shine in our hearts so we could know the glory of God that is seen in the face of Jesus Christ. We now have this light shining in our hearts, but we ourselves are like fragile clay jars containing this great treasure. This makes it clear that our great power is from God, not from ourselves.

Even when we feel fragile and broken, and even despite all we have lost, we can still contain the greatest treasure of all: our faith in Jesus.

When I lost Natalie and Noah, I lost the close relationship I had with my friend among many other things as a result. Loss changes things and that is the reality. But the most important reality of all is that Christ's sufficiency for us will never change, never be lost, and never fail. Though it may feel as though we *have nothing*, we can still *possess everything*. I pray that you will carry this truth with you today and always.

Journal entry from July 28, 2017

Father, it's been six weeks since Natalie died. Tomorrow will be six weeks since Noah. These have been the hardest six weeks of my life, filled with more pain than I've experienced in my whole life combined. Father, I believe You're working in this whirlwind and in this storm. As I read this morning about David and Bathsheba losing their baby and then having Solomon born to them soon afterward, I can't help but find hope in that. I know You don't always work the same for and in everyone's lives, but You are always faithful and I have seen You use such horrible situations and bring good out of them. Father, I believe that for my life and for Natalie and Noah's deaths. Give me eyes to see You working, give me wisdom to stay in Your will, and show me what You want from me and from this. Father, I'm Yours. I'm wholly surrendered, and I've learned through this in a tangible way that my life would be dark and hopeless without Your light and love. I've learned that in spite of my circumstances, I will continue to worship You and thank You—not for what You give me or do for me, but for who You are and because You are deserving of my praise no matter what is going on around me. Lord, You have to be my everything. Amen.

When the storms of life come, the wicked are whirled away,
but the godly have a lasting foundation.

—Proverbs 10:25 (NLT)

CHAPTER 20

BECAUSE OF THE ROCK

And the rain fell, and the floods and torrents came,
and the winds blew and slammed against that house;
yet it did not fall because it had been founded on the rock.

—Matthew 7:25 (AMP)

In Matthew 7, Jesus tells a parable of a wise man who built his house on rock and a foolish man who built his house on sand. As we read in the verse above, the wise man's house is able to survive the fierce storm because of its strong foundation. Conversely for the foolish man, verse 27 (AMP) tells us,

And the rain fell, and the floods and torrents came,
and the winds blew and slammed against that house;
and it fell—and great and complete was its fall.

Unlike the house built on rock, the house built on sand did not have a solid foundation that could withstand the rains, floods, and winds.

Does the storm depicted in this parable sound like what has happened in your life? *The rain fell, the floods and torrents came, and the winds blew and slammed.* That's what it felt like for me—like any and all calm, peace, and stability in my life were gone. And the storm I was facing threatened to absolutely break me just as the storm did to the house built on sand. Without a strong foundation on Jesus, it would have.

This parable depicts how a life that is not built first and foremost on Jesus will not be able to withstand the storms that come. Without Him as the rock of our lives, we are not standing on anything that can uphold us, sustain us, or steady us. As David writes in Psalm 62:2 (NLT),

> He alone is my rock and my salvation, my fortress where I will never be shaken.

And in Psalm 18:2 (NLT), he writes,

> The Lord is my rock, my fortress, and my savior; my God is my rock, in whom I find protection. He is my shield, the power that saves me, and my place of safety.

The apostle Paul also speaks of Christ as the rock in 1 Corinthians 10:1–4 (NLT):

> I don't want you to forget, dear brothers and sisters, about our ancestors in the wilderness long ago. All of them were guided by a cloud that moved ahead of them, and all of them walked through the sea on dry ground. In the cloud and in the sea, all of them were baptized as followers of Moses. All of them ate the same spiritual food, and all of them drank the same spiritual water. For they drank from the spiritual rock that traveled with them, and *that rock was Christ* [emphasis mine].

Paul is referencing here the Israelites' time of wandering in the wilderness and how God guided them, made a way for them when there was no way, provided manna and quail for them to eat, and miraculously gave them water from the rock. And then he says, "And that rock was Christ." The rock that gave them life-sustaining water is a symbol of Christ the Rock, who is the sustainer of our lives each day as well. The Israelites would not have survived their wilderness without water provided by the rock, and in our desperate circumstances, we won't make it through either without the hope, grace, strength, purpose, and mercy provided by Christ our Rock.

If you ever wonder how it is that so many people who do not know Jesus survive the tragedies they face, as I mentioned in a previous chapter, I have wondered the same thing. I think in those cases their physical lives may go on, yes, but there may be things in their lives that *don't* survive: I think their joy may not survive, or their peace, or their hope. And worst of all in many cases, I fear that the salvation of their souls may not survive.

Just like the foundation on rock made all the difference in the house's ability to withstand the storm in Matthew 7, so Jesus does for our lives.

So what does having our foundation set on Jesus look like practically? The apostle Jude gives us instruction on this in Jude 1:20–21 (NIV):

> But you, dear friends, by building yourselves up in your most holy faith and praying in the Holy Spirit, keep yourselves in God's love as you wait for the mercy of our Lord Jesus Christ to bring you to eternal life.

Build yourselves up in your faith. Pray in the Holy Spirit. Keep yourselves in God's love. Build upon the foundation we have set on Jesus by growing in our knowledge and our faith; invest in and deepen our prayer life; and remain, rest, and rely on God's love.

The apostle Paul also tells us in 1 Corinthians 3:10–11 (NIV),

> By the grace God has given me, I laid a foundation
> as a wise builder, and someone else is building on
> it. But each one should build with care. For no one
> can lay any foundation other than the one already
> laid, which is Jesus Christ.

Paul is describing here how his preaching of the gospel has laid a foundation on Jesus Christ and how as the church grows, others will be building upon that foundation. As a result, he is warning those who are building upon it to "build with care" because there is *no solid foundation* other than Jesus. Faith in Jesus is the foundation of the good news of the gospel—no ifs, ands, or buts—just as faith in Jesus is the foundation that sets the structure of who we are, how we live, and why we are able to persevere through life's greatest pains.

Having this foundation on Jesus doesn't mean that we won't be afflicted by our devastating circumstances. The house built on the rock in Matthew 7 still had to experience the pressure of the rains, withstand the rising waters, and feel the winds slamming against it. Maybe it lost a few shingles or maybe the siding got damaged, but *it did not fall.* The storm tested the strength of the house's foundation just as the tragedies in our lives test ours.

As it was for the house built on the rock, may that be true of you and me—that as we deal with the pain of our circumstances and the brokenness of our lives, we ultimately do not fall into bitterness, hopelessness, loss of purpose, or worst of all, faithlessness. In the midst of our heartbreak, may our foundation remain strongly set on Jesus the rock.

Journal entry from July 29, 2017

Father, all my hope is in You, and even now, I believe You're working and I will worship You. Thank You for the peace and strength that You give in the midst of tragedy. You are my strong fortress, and I need You and seek You to make my way perfect. You are my God, the only one and true God. Thank You for the strength You give to my weak body and spirit. Father, thank You for everything You've given and provided in my life for I know and profess that all I have is from You and by Your grace, not my own doing. I need You every second of every day. I build my life on You, Jesus, because if I didn't, I wouldn't be still standing at all. Be my rock, my firm foundation, and uphold me. Amen.

I cling to you;
your strong right hand
holds me securely.

—Psalm 63:8 (NLT)

CHAPTER 21

I STILL BELIEVE

I would have despaired had I not believed
that I would see the goodness of the Lord in the land of the living.
Wait for and confidently expect the Lord;
be strong and let your heart take courage;
yes, wait for and confidently expect the Lord.

—Psalm 27:13–14 (AMP)

The apostle Paul lived a tough life. For him, as for many others, becoming a follower of Christ did not lead to a life of luxury, ease, or safety—just the opposite actually. And yet, every time I read through the book of 2 Corinthians, I am amazed by his commitment to follow Jesus no matter the cost. He writes of some of the hardships he endured in 2 Corinthians 11:24–27 (NLT):

> Five different times the Jewish leaders gave me thirty-nine lashes. Three times I was beaten with rods. Once I was stoned. Three times I was shipwrecked. Once I spent a whole night and a day adrift at sea. I have traveled on many long journeys. I have faced danger from rivers and from robbers. I have faced

danger from my own people, the Jews, as well as from the Gentiles. I have faced danger in the cities, in the deserts, and on the seas. And I have faced danger from men who claim to be believers but are not. I have worked hard and long, enduring many sleepless nights. I have been hungry and thirsty and have often gone without food. I have shivered in the cold, without enough clothing to keep me warm.

Facing just one of these hardships would be challenging. But all of them? Wouldn't being shipwrecked once be enough? Yet he says he was shipwrecked three times. Wouldn't facing dangers from rivers and robbers be enough? Yet he says he also faced dangers from the Jews, the Gentiles, in the cities, in the deserts, and on the seas. It doesn't seem quite fair, does it? Especially for someone who is walking in the will of God. Shouldn't there come a point when enough is enough? When someone has experienced enough pain and should be guarded against having to experience any more? As evidenced by Paul's life and many others, life oftentimes just doesn't work that way.

Just over two years after Natalie and Noah's deaths, I was absolutely ecstatic to be pregnant again. I felt beyond grateful and humbled by God's mercy on me. I fell in love all over again with the tiny life inside me as two separate ultrasounds each showed a strong heartbeat and a healthy growing baby. All the excitement, anticipation, hope, and love welled up within me. *This time is going to be different*, I thought.

At just about ten weeks into my pregnancy, I felt a strong sense of peace going into my third ultrasound—but that sense of peace did not last long. The ultrasound started, and there was my baby.

But no movement.

No heartbeat.

No life.

My baby had died—again.

All at once, all the emotions, pain, panic, and fear that I experienced after Natalie and Noah's deaths came rushing back. It was as if that deep wound that had begun to heal was all of a sudden ripped back open. I was hysterical. I was in shock. I was in unimaginable pain.

My immediate emotional response was to repeatedly cry out *"No!"* as if to say, "No, God, this can't happen again. No, God, I don't want this. No, God, I can't do this again. No, God, just no!" It was a response of defiance. Questions began to rush through my mind.

Why would He let my baby die, again?

Why did I have three babies in heaven when He knew how desperately I wanted to be a mom, to have a full family?

Why would He allow this much pain to come into my life, again?

As I sat there on the exam table, tears streaming down my face, heartbroken, scared, and hurting, I realized that I once again was facing a critical decision: was I going to choose to trust God again? Or was I going to turn my back on Him this time?

As I got up from the exam table to get dressed, I firmly said to Jason in between tears and grief-stricken breaths, "I love the Lord, and He has been so good to me."

At that moment, I willed myself to praise the Lord. I did not feel like it. I did not even want to. But I knew that I needed to.

I poured my heart out to One who once again held my baby in His arms, as if to say, "Though I don't feel the comfort of Your presence now, Father, I will lift my eyes to You and profess Your faithfulness. Though nothing around me makes sense, I will trust You. Though I'm in pain that I think may kill me, I will praise You. Though I'm scared and angry and hurt, I will not run from You. I will press into You, not because I feel like it, but because You and only You are the way, the truth, and the life. You and only You are my God, my Savior, the One to whom I owe everything."

I chose to believe that God is worthy of my praise, trust, and adoration even when I didn't feel like giving Him those things.

I chose to believe in the goodness of His character even though I could find no goodness in what I was facing.

I chose to believe that He is God, my loving Father and Savior of my soul, and that fact is not negated by the pain I may experience in this life.

David writes in Psalm 27:13 (AMP),

> I would have despaired had I not believed that I would see the goodness of the Lord in the land of the living.

And I too would have succumbed to despair had I not believed that God was *still* good.

I had experienced God's sustaining grace, comfort, mercy, and compassion poured out over me after I lost Natalie and Noah. I had experienced His enduring goodness in the midst of my darkest days. And I believed that I would experience it again as my life fell to pieces once more.

The apostle Paul too, after all the hardships and pain that he faced, demonstrates a faith-filled perspective gained only by personal experience. In 2 Corinthians 12:9–10 (NLT), Paul writes,

> So now I am glad to boast about my weaknesses, so that the power of Christ can work through me. That's why I take pleasure in my weaknesses, and in the insults, hardships, persecutions, and troubles that I suffer for Christ. For when I am weak, then I am strong.

Paul's attitude is just the opposite of one who has become bitter and shakes his fist at God with an "enough is enough" attitude. In spite of all his sufferings, he *chose* to submit to God as Lord of his life. *For when I am weak, then I am strong*, he says. I have learned and experienced the truth of this remarkable reality as well.

Is life hard a lot of the time? Yes, it is. Is life fair all the time? Not at all. But faith in Jesus Christ is not defined by or dependent upon the ease and fairness of life. Rather, faith in Jesus Christ is defined by and dependent upon the belief of what Jesus did on the cross for me and you, the belief in the loving and good nature of God, the belief in His supremacy and sovereignty, and the belief in His second coming, to name a few.

And, dear Heavenly Father, I still believe.

Father, I'm in pain this morning, and I don't understand. I don't understand why this baby had to die, why this happened. Father, I'm hurting so badly from it. You know how much I wanted this baby, how thankful I was, and how humbled I was by Your loving kindness poured out over me in the provision of this baby. Father, I don't know what to do now. I want these losses and this pain to mean something, to have purpose, to be used. Father, please use this in my life for Your glory to help others and to point people to You. In my confusion and pain, I look to You, the One to whom I owe everything. And I choose to trust You even when I am hit again with the greatest sadness and disappointment that I could imagine. I choose to trust You now and every day and to proclaim that You are good. O Father, You have been my refuge and my strong tower. Please help me. Thank You for all You've given me and all You've done. Thank You for how You're moving now even though I can't see it. Thank You that You are Almighty God, that nothing is too hard for You, that You know the plans You have for me, that You love me, and are for me. You are my God. And, Lord, in this life I choose You and will follow You. Amen.

He reached down from heaven and rescued me;
he drew me out of deep waters.
He led me to a place of safety;
he rescued me because he delights in me.
God's way is perfect.
All the Lord's promises prove true.
He is a shield for all who look to him for protection.
For who is God except the Lord?
Who but our God is a solid rock?
God is my strong fortress,
and he makes my way perfect.

—2 Samuel 22:17, 22:20, 22:31–33 (NLT)

CHAPTER 22

Seeing How

Then I said to you, "Do not be terrified; do not be afraid
of them. The Lord your God, who is going before you,
will fight for you, as he did for you in Egypt, before your
very eyes, and in the wilderness. There you saw how the
Lord your God carried you, as a father carries his son,
all the way you went until you reached this place."

—Deuteronomy 1:29–31 (NIV)

He has watched your every step through this great
wilderness. During these forty years, the Lord your God
has been with you, and you have lacked nothing.

—Deuteronomy 2:7 (NLT)

In Deuteronomy 1 (NIV), the Israelites find themselves at the edge
of the Promised Land after many long hard years of journeying.
Before they enter to claim this inheritance that God had promised,
Moses addresses the people to remind them of all that God had
done for them and to encourage them to renew their commitment
to God's covenant.

The Israelites' journey to the Promised Land gave them the

unique (and difficult) opportunity to get to know and experience God in ways they never would have otherwise. During their time in the wilderness, they faced danger, possible starvation and dehydration, exhaustion, fear, and many trials. Yet Moses reminds them in Deuteronomy 1:31 that during that time,

> There *you saw how* [emphasis mine] the Lord your God carried you, as a father carries his son, all the way you went until you reached this place.

Through their hardships, they experienced God carrying them through it—He provided for them, He sustained them, He fought for them, He led them, and He never left them on their own.

As a loving father would care for and carry his son, so He did for the Israelites in the wilderness. As challenging and arduous as their journey was, without all those years spent there, they would not have come to know God as provider, sustainer, protector, and leader. They would not have come to know Him as the father that He is.

This is true for you and me as well. Our losses can enable us to know and experience God on a far deeper level. In the midst of our grief, we find ourselves in desperate need of help, comfort, hope, guidance, provision, strength, and sustenance. And all these things we will find in Him. I want to highlight again what Moses says to the Israelites in verse 31—*there* (meaning in the wilderness) *you saw how* ... And *here* we will see how. *Here* in our heartbreak, we won't have to read about who God is or learn about Him from a sermon. We won't have to blindly believe in Him and who He is. Because *here* we will *see* how He carries us through.

Every day, I still miss my babies and wonder who they would have been. After all these years, I am still pained by my losses. But also through all these years, I have *seen* God show up for me. I have *seen* Him carry me all the way I went until I reached this place—and I could not have reached this place without Him. A place where despite my pain I can live each day in the fullness of His joy and peace. A place where, despite the tears I still cry, I am not utterly consumed by my grief. A place where, despite my lack of answers as to why my babies died, I trust God and love Him even more than I did before I lost them. I have had the opportunity to experience the depths of His grace, mercy, and love and to really know Him. And for that, I am grateful.

Weeks, months, or years from now, I pray that you will look back too and see how He carried you.

Journal entry from November 23, 2019

Father, my heart is hurting. It feels like it's broken in two. My broken heart I set on You and trust You to heal it. O Father, I miss my baby. I miss all my babies. Sometimes I feel like throwing a temper tantrum like a little girl, and sometimes I feel like begging You. But, Lord, I will resist doing those things and will choose to trust You and Your word—that You work all things for the good of those who love You and are called according to Your purpose for them, that You know the plans You have for me, that You love me, and that You know the desires of my heart. Thank You that You are the restorer, the redeemer, and the healer. Please, Father, show Yourself to me as all those things. Though I feel like I am once again sitting in darkness, please be my light. Please carry me through and sustain me. And, Father, I will proclaim Your goodness even as my heart is broken. Help me. Amen.

Be merciful to me, Lord, for I am in distress;
my eyes grow weak with sorrow,
my soul and body with grief.
My life is consumed by anguish
and my years by groaning;
my strength fails because of my affliction,
and my bones grow weak.
But I trust in you, Lord;
I say, "You are my God."
My times are in your hands.

—Psalm 31:9–10, 31:14–15 (NIV)

CHAPTER 23

WHAT THE LOCUSTS TOOK

I will repay you for the years the locusts have eaten—
the great locust and the young locust, the other locusts
and the locust swarm—my great army that I sent among
you. You will have plenty to eat, until you are full, and
you will praise the name of the Lord your God, who has
worked wonders for you; never again will my people be
shamed. Then you will know that I am in Israel, that I
am the Lord your God, and that there is no other.

—Joel 2:25–27 (NIV)

In the book of Joel, the prophet Joel speaks of a great locust plague that has savaged the Kingdom of Judah. In Joel 1:4 (NLT), we read,

> After the cutting locusts finished eating the crops, the swarming locusts took what was left! After them came the hopping locusts, and then the stripping locusts, too!

This locust swarm had devastating effects on the area's agriculture and farmers; every kind of plant crop and food had been destroyed, resulting in a lack of supply of agricultural offerings for the Temple in Jerusalem.

Joel speaks of the devastation in verses 11–12 (NLT):

> Despair, all you farmers! Wail, all you vine growers! Weep, because the wheat and barley—all the crops of the field—are ruined. The grapevines have dried up, and the fig trees have withered. The pomegranate trees, palm trees, and apple trees—all the fruit trees—have dried up. *And the people's joy has dried up with them* [emphasis mine].

The locusts had come upon the Kingdom of Judah, destroying everything in their path and stealing the people's livelihoods, physical and emotional well-being, and even their spiritual security. Doesn't loss feel like this to some extent too?

After Natalie and Noah's bodies were each taken, all I had left of them were the blankets they had been wrapped in and the hats they had worn. I immediately became irrationally attached to those pieces of fabric. They never left my grasp—I carried them with me throughout the house, took them to bed with me, and brought them with me in the car. It felt like those pieces of fabric were all that survived the devastation of what had happened in my life— like the locusts had come and savaged everything else. The empty bassinets in Natalie and Noah's nursery had once filled me with such expectancy, excitement, joy, and gratefulness. Now they just filled me with pain. Their room and even my body, which had before felt so full of life, felt so very empty. The locusts had come. And they had wreaked havoc in my life and every aspect of my well-being.

Two and a half years later after my third loss, it felt like the locusts were back—once again destroying my hopes and breaking my heart back into pieces. Two days after my D&C, I read Joel 2:25 (NIV), and it seemed to jump off the page:

> I will repay you for the years the locusts have eaten.

Some other translations use the word *restore* in place of *repay*. The Message version says it like this:

> I'll make up for the years of the locust, the great locust devastation …

This verse comes after Joel's urging of the people to lament, repent of their rebellion, and return wholeheartedly to God. God's response to them in verse 25 demonstrates the depths of His mercy, kindness, and generosity toward His people. He promises the people of Judah that years of abundant harvests would follow the years of devastation that the locusts had caused. Joel 2:24 (NLT) says,

> The threshing floors will again be piled high with grain, and the presses will overflow with new wine and olive oil.

God then says in verse 26,

> Once again you will have all the food you want, and you will praise the Lord your God, who does these miracles for you.

What a gracious God He is!

Immediately after I read Joel 2:25, it became my prayer. I prayed that God would restore the years the locusts had eaten in my life—that He would restore all the tears I had cried, all the pain, and all the loss that had taken so much from me. Not because I deserved it or was worthy of His mercy and kindness, but because I believed

He could and knew He was the *only* one who could. It was not meant as a prayer of demand or defiance, but rather a prayer of utter dependence.

I recognize that the years the locusts have eaten cannot be fully restored in our earthly lives, but there are things that God can restore here and now. How exactly He chooses to accomplish that may look different for each of us, but for all of us, I know that He can restore our joy, peace, sense of purpose, fruitfulness, vision, hope, faith, and devotion to Him. For as much as we've lost, He can fill our lives richly with Himself.

Psalm 86:15–16 (NLT) says,

> But you, O Lord, are a God of compassion and mercy, slow to get angry and filled with unfailing love and faithfulness. Look down and have mercy on me. Give your strength to your servant …

He is a God of kindness, mercy, compassion, and grace. May He have mercy on us and give us strength today, and may He restore to us the years the locusts have eaten in accordance with His will for our lives.

Journal entry from November 24, 2019

Father, I feel like the locusts have eaten a few years from me … I feel sad, confused, and not sure what to do now. I feel empty now with no baby within me again. O Lord, will You repay me for the years the locusts have eaten? Not because I deserve it. Not because I am good, but because of who You are. You are good. You are the Restorer, and I trust my life to You. And, Father, I trust not in what You do, but in who You are. Father, I feel hurt, but help me to honor You in this. Thank You that You see me; I need to be seen by You and to be held by You—to be carried by You. I know not what to do but my eyes are on You. You are my God, and You always will be. You are so worthy of praise, honor, and glory. Even when I can't see You, I will trust You. Even when I can't feel You, I will trust You. I love You, Lord. Amen.

"Set My Heart"
Lyrics by Vertical Worship

Quiet the voice of doubt again,
Echo within me every promise,
Let your Word be louder than my fears.
Speak to the void when I can't see,
Lift up my head in every valley,
Let your joy be greater than my grief.

I have set my heart,
Set my, set my heart on You.
You have every part of me,
I set my heart on You.

You make a way when none is found,
You tell the roaring ocean to bow.
I believe You're moving even now,
Right here, right now.

I have set my heart,
Set my, set my heart on You.
You have every part of me,
I set my heart on You.

I have set my heart,
Set my, set my heart on You.
You have every part of me,
I set my heart on You.
I set my, set my heart on You.

Nothing will ever break me, ever slay me,
All my hope in You.
Nothing will ever shake me, overtake me,
All my hope in You.

Nothing will ever break me, ever slay me,
All my hope in You.
Nothing will ever shake me, overtake me,
All my hope in You.

CHAPTER 24

LESSONS FROM HANNAH

Hear my prayer, Lord;
listen to my cry for mercy.
When I am in distress, I call to you,
because you answer me.

—Psalm 86:6–7 (NIV)

Hannah's story in 1 Samuel has resonated with me for as long as I can remember. Through my years of infertility and multiple losses, it is one I have been drawn back to and found hope from time and time again.

We read in 1 Samuel chapter 1 (NLT) about a man named Elkanah who had two wives, Hannah and Peninnah. Peninnah had been able to bear children for Elkanah, but Hannah had not. Like most other women experiencing infertility, Hannah was pained and distressed about her inability to conceive.

In compliance with the law of Moses at the time, each year Elkanah and his family would travel to the Tabernacle in Shiloh to worship and bring sacrifices to God. As they traveled, 1 Samuel 1:6–7 tells us,

> So Peninnah would taunt Hannah and make fun of her because the Lord had kept her from having children. Year after year it was the same—Peninnah would taunt Hannah as they went to the Tabernacle. Each time, Hannah would be reduced to tears and would not even eat.

After one of these sacrificial meals at Shiloh, Hannah leaves in deep anguish to go and pray. She cries out bitterly to God and prays,

> O Lord of Heaven's Armies, if you will look upon my sorrow and answer my prayer and give me a son, then I will give him back to you. (1 Samuel 1:11)

The next day after worshipping the Lord once more, Elkanah and his family return to their home and the Lord remembers Hannah's plea. Verse 20 tells us that in due time she gives birth to a son and names him Samuel, which sounds similar to the Hebrew term for "asked of God."

After Samuel had been weaned, which in that culture was usually not until two or three years of age, Hannah takes him to the Tabernacle in Shiloh along with other sacrificial offerings. She brings the boy to Eli the priest and says,

> I am the very woman who stood here several years ago praying to the Lord. I asked the Lord to give me this boy, and he has granted my request. Now I am giving him to the Lord, and he will belong to the Lord his whole life. (1 Samuel 1:26–28)

Elkanah and Hannah then return to their home, leaving Samuel there to serve the Lord.

I find it easy to imagine how painful this must have been for Hannah to do. As she left Samuel at the Tabernacle in fulfillment of her vow to God, she lost the lifetime she could have had raising him. Her choice to follow through with her vow despite this great cost demonstrates extraordinary faithfulness to God.

Later on, in 1 Samuel 2:19, we read that each year when Hannah and Elkanah return to Shiloh, Hannah brings Samuel a small, handmade coat. Verses 20–21 tells us,

> Before they returned home, Eli would bless Elkanah and his wife and say, "May the Lord give you other children to take the place of this one she gave to the Lord." And the Lord blessed Hannah, and she conceived and gave birth to three sons and two daughters. Meanwhile, Samuel grew up in the presence of the Lord.

If you're not yet sure where I'm going with this as you sit there mourning your loss, hang in there with me. The story of Hannah doesn't serve as a one-size-fits-all promise that God will also give us three sons and two daughters following our losses, but it does serve as a rich illustration of who God is.

First, we see the demonstration of God's graciousness and kindness to us in our anguish. In 1 Samuel 1:10, it says,

> Hannah was in deep anguish, crying bitterly as she prayed to the Lord.

The Lord not only remembers the prayer she cried out to Him that night, He answers it. He steps into Hannah's barrenness like only He can do and gives life. He hears her, and He heals her.

He doesn't leave her in the depths of her desperation; rather, He responds with miraculous provision.

God looks upon us in our anguish today with that same graciousness and kindness. 2 Corinthians 1:3 (NLT) tells us,

> God is our merciful Father and the God of all comfort.

The end result of our stories may look different from Hannah's, but *He* never changes or casts a shifting shadow (James 1:17). He is the same God to us now as He was to Hannah—gracious, kind, merciful, and faithful.

The second point to pull out from Hannah's story is that God works through painful circumstances. As Hannah traveled to Shiloh to give up her one and only son to spend the rest of his life serving at the Tabernacle, I doubt that she had any idea how incredibly God was going to use him throughout his lifetime. I would imagine she was too overcome by her grief at the time to envision how her son could grow into a renowned man of God, which he did.

Samuel became a great prophet, was Israel's last and possibly greatest judge, anointed the very first kings of Israel (Saul and David), and was known for his unrelenting obedience to God. Throughout his lifetime, God spoke through him to call the Israelites to return to the Lord and used him to prepare the nation of Israel for some of its greatest decades under the kingships of David and Solomon.

Hannah's loss certainly was different from yours and mine; hers was an intentional giving up of her son to fulfill her vow to God. I do imagine though that, like our losses, hers was also unwanted and painful. Yet through her loss, God worked. He took that small child who had been dedicated to Him in the most literal way and turned Him into a great prophet whom He used to accomplish His will for the nation of Israel.

Just as God worked through Hannah's loss, He works through ours as well. James 1:12 (ESV) tells us,

Blessed is the man who remains steadfast under trial, for when he has stood the test he will receive the crown of life, which God has promised to those who love him.

2 Corinthians 4:16–18 (ESV) encourages,

So we do not lose heart. Though our outer self is wasting away, our inner self is being renewed day by day. For this light momentary affliction is preparing for us an eternal weight of glory beyond all comparison, as we look not to the things that are seen but to the things that are unseen. For the things that are seen are transient, but the things that are unseen are eternal.

And 2 Corinthians 1:3–4 (ESV) says,

Blessed be the God and Father of our Lord Jesus Christ, the Father of mercies and God of all comfort, who comforts us in all our affliction, so that we may be able to comfort those who are in any affliction, with the comfort with which we ourselves are comforted by God.

Out of Hannah's loss came one of Israel's greatest prophets. And He can make *something* come out of ours.

The last (and maybe my favorite) facet of God that I want to highlight from Hannah's story is His faithfulness. He answers Hannah's initial prayer for a son in accordance with His will for Samuel's life, but He doesn't stop there. He goes on to bless Hannah with three more sons and two daughters after the years of infertility she experienced and the loss, in a sense, of her first son.

Through this, we see His faithfulness to respond to the cries of His people.

We see His faithfulness to provide and bring comfort.

We see His faithfulness to show up, not leave us on our own, and intercede in dire circumstances.

How exactly He chooses to demonstrate His faithfulness to us may look different than it did for Hannah, but He *will* demonstrate it. 2 Timothy 2:13 (NLT) tells us,

> If we are unfaithful, he remains faithful, for he cannot deny who he is.

He is the same God today as He was yesterday, which means that He is the same God today as He was three thousand or more years ago to Hannah. Our circumstance isn't the same as Hannah's, I know, but our God is the same.

His compassion, ability to work through the most painful experiences, and His faithfulness are absolute and unfailing. Even when everything around us is changing, transient, and disappointing, He's not.

In 1 Samuel 2:1–10, we read Hannah's prayer of praise to God, in which she prays *before* God's gracious provision of more children to her. May we praise God today as Hannah did, not necessarily for what He's done for us yet in the midst of our losses, but just for who He is:

> My heart rejoices in the Lord!
>   The Lord has made me strong.
> Now I have an answer for my enemies;
>   I rejoice because you rescued me.
> No one is holy like the Lord!
>   There is no one besides you;
>   there is no Rock like our God.
> The childless woman now has seven children,

and the woman with many children wastes away.
The Lord gives both death and life;
  he brings some down to the grave but raises
  others up.
The Lord makes some poor and others rich;
  he brings some down and lifts others up.
He lifts the poor from the dust
  and the needy from the garbage dump.
He sets them among princes,
  placing them in seats of honor.
For all the earth is the Lord's,
  and he has set the world in order.
He will protect his faithful ones,
  but the wicked will disappear in darkness.
No one will succeed by strength alone.
Those who fight against the Lord will be shattered.
He thunders against them from heaven;
  the Lord judges throughout the earth.
He gives power to his king;
  he increases the strength of his anointed one.

    —1 Samuel 2:1–2, 2:5–10 (NLT)

Father, I seek You. Would You please draw near to me as I try to draw near to You? Lord, I recognize my desperate need for You, and I will myself to rejoice in You no matter the circumstances around me. Father, I feel so sad and feel like I'm waking up each day into a bad dream rather than waking up from one. Father, I wanted that baby. I loved that baby. And yet, that baby was Yours long before it was ever mine. I know that baby was merely lent to me to be a steward of. Father, please see my heart. I feel scared not knowing anything about what's to come, but I place my fears at Your altar, trusting in Your promises, trusting that You are a good God, that You are my Father, that Your heart mourns with me and grieves as I grieve. You have been so good to me, and I trust it all to You, for where else would I place my trust? You are my portion and You are my strength. Father, would You please redeem these tragedies in my life? In my struggling, I seek You. Amen.

We went through fire and through water,
Yet You brought us out into a [broad]
place of abundance [to be refreshed].
—Psalm 66:12 (AMP)

CHAPTER 25

CARRYING THE WEIGHT

Then Jesus said, "Come to me, all of you who are weary
and carry heavy burdens, and I will give you rest. Take my
yoke upon you. Let me teach you, because I am humble and
gentle at heart, and you will find rest for your souls. For my
yoke is easy to bear, and the burden I give you is light."

—Matthew 11:28–30 (NLT)

The classic song "You Are My Sunshine" has been widely popular since
the 1940s—it is a well-known children's lullaby and one of the most
repeatedly recorded songs in American popular music, having been
covered by many big-time artists. It is one of those songs that is easy
to get stuck in your head and that most people know the chorus to:

> You are my sunshine
> My only sunshine
> You make me happy
> When skies are gray
> You'll never know, dear
> How much I love you
> Please don't take
> My sunshine away

This song is one that I have sung on a regular basis to each of the three children God has given me after my losses. There are a few versions of the song that are composed of differing verses, but the one that I am most familiar with has a verse that goes like this:

The other night, dear
As I lay sleeping
I dreamed I held you
In my arms
When I awoke, dear
I was mistaken
So I hung my head and I cried

I typically sing just the chorus to my kids, but as that verse runs through my mind each time, I always think of Natalie, Noah, and the third baby I never got to meet. It holds a certain heaviness in my heart that way—but singing this song over the years has been a way that I carry my three children in heaven with me in my everyday life now as I care for their siblings.

As the years have gone by, the pain has not gone away, but I have learned how to carry it and how to carry them with me. Loss is a lifelong burden—a heavy one—but it is not something that we have to or are even supposed to carry on our own. In Matthew 11:28 (NLT), Jesus says,

Come to me, all of you who are weary and carry heavy burdens, and I will give you rest. Take my yoke upon you. Let me teach you, because I am humble and gentle at heart, and you will find rest for your souls. For my yoke is easy to bear, and the burden I give you is light.

When Jesus said this, He was referring to the yoke of slavery resulting from the legalistic religion practiced by the Pharisees. The

Pharisees' codification of all the rules and regulations stipulated in the old Mosaic law had become burdensome, focused on externalism, and even oppressive. In Matthew 23:3 (NLT), Jesus says,

> They [the Pharisees] crush people with unbearable religious demands and never lift a finger to ease the burden.

Not to say that the Old Testament law wasn't good and holy, because it was, but its dependence on a person's works made it unable to truly liberate people from their sins. Jesus is saying in Matthew 11:28 that through Him (Jesus) there is freedom from the law and rest for the soul. The heavy burden caused by legalistic religion is lifted by faith in Jesus.

Similarly, when we lay the heavy burdens of our losses before Jesus, He frees us from enslavement to our pain and gives us rest too. The pain doesn't go away, no, but in Him, it's not quite as heavy to carry.

In Jeremiah 31:25 (ESV), the Lord says, "For I will satisfy the weary soul, and every languishing soul I will replenish."

So how exactly do we lay our burdens down to Him? Jesus gives us the answer in Matthew 11:28 when He says, "Come to me."

That's really it. Come to Him. The person of Jesus. Believe in Him, live for Him, love Him, seek Him, trust Him. As you lay yourself before Him, all your burdens you lay down in the process. Just as two oxen being yoked together lightens the burden of the load they're carrying, being yoked together continually to Jesus lightens ours as well. The burden isn't necessarily lifted, but we're no longer carrying it on our own.

He is humble, He is gentle, and He teaches us what we need to learn to carry our losses through our lives without being crushed by the weight of it.

For me now, as heavy as the weight is, I can sing "You Are My

Sunshine" to my children without absolutely falling apart every time because He gives me the grace to do so. And as I recount that verse,

> The other night, dear
> As I lay sleeping
> I dreamed I held you
> In my arms
> When I awoke, dear
> I was mistaken
> So I hung my head and I cried

I can carry the weight of it because He helps me to.

Journal entry from November 28, 2019

Father, on this Thanksgiving morning without my sweet baby with me, and without Natalie and Noah here with me, I want to first and foremost just thank You. Thank You that You are with me, that You go before me, that You fight for me, that You're working in ways I cannot see, that You're my defender, redeemer, restorer, and the lifter of my head. You are my rock and fortress. Father, You know where I'm at and what I'm struggling with, and this morning, I'm not going to ask You for anything. I'm just going to praise You. Father, I praise You and I worship You for who You are. I bow down before You, the worthy King, with my life submitted to You, with my pain in Your hands to be used for what You want. I stand still before You this morning, trusting that You're working, that You're for me, that You've saved me, and that this pain and heartache won't be wasted. I need You, draw near to You, and humble myself before You. Amen.

Come and listen, all you who fear God,
and I will tell you what he did for me.
For I cried out to him for help,
praising him as I spoke.
Praise God, who did not ignore my prayer
or withdraw his unfailing love from me.

—Psalm 66:16–17, 66:20 (NLT)

CHAPTER 26

NO TURNING BACK

For you know that the testing of
your faith produces steadfastness.

—James 1:3 (ESV)

Losing Natalie and Noah was by far the hardest and most painful experience of my life. It is the pivotal crisis that partitioned how I think about my life now into two parts: before Natalie and Noah's loss, and after it. It drove me nearly to my breaking point and tested my faith in a literal way.

After my third loss, it felt as though I was being tested all over again. It didn't seem fair, and I know that I'll never understand the whys on this side of heaven, but I also know that going through another devastating experience gave me the opportunity once again to demonstrate what was really in my heart. It gave me the opportunity once more to choose between turning away from God or solidifying the steadfastness of my belief.

My faith has been tested, yes. Was it hard? Very. But through that testing, I am more convinced than ever that Jesus is who He says He is.

The Message version of James 1:2–4 says,

You know that under pressure, your faith-life is forced into the open and shows its true colors … Let it do its work so you become mature and well-developed, not deficient in any way.

Romans 5:3–4 (NLT) also says,

For we know that [problems and trials] help us develop endurance. And endurance develops strength of character, and character strengthens our confident hope of salvation.

The greatest trials of my life have become my greatest testimony of God's grace, mercy, and faithfulness.

One of the most important truths that I learned from my losses, and that I want to reiterate, is that love for God needs to be based on who He is—not on what He gives us, what He does or does not do for us, or how good our circumstances are. God is worthy of our love, praise, and adoration because He is Lord of lords, King of kings, and Savior of the world. He is worthy of our devotion and worship *always*.

His faithfulness doesn't change even when our circumstances may try to tell us that it has. He is God, and He is good. He is God, and He is worthy. He is God, and I will live my life devoted to Him and His kingdom. Through Jesus, He has saved me from my sins and offers eternal life to me though I've done nothing to deserve it. Even when everything in this life is falling apart, His saving grace still stands.

At Natalie and Noah's memorial service, one of the songs that Jason and I chose to be played was the old hymn "I Have Decided to Follow Jesus." It is a song that I go back to often, especially when I am feeling weighed down by life's heartaches. The lyrics read as follows:

I have decided to follow Jesus;
I have decided to follow Jesus;
I have decided to follow Jesus;
No turning back, no turning back.
The world behind me, the cross before me;
The world behind me, the cross before me;
The world behind me, the cross before me;
No turning back, no turning back.
Though none go with me, still I will follow;
Though none go with me, still I will follow;
Though none go with me, still I will follow;
No turning back, no turning back.
My cross I'll carry, till I see Jesus;
My cross I'll carry, till I see Jesus;
My cross I'll carry, till I see Jesus;
No turning back, no turning back.
Will you decide now to follow Jesus?
Will you decide now to follow Jesus?
Will you decide now to follow Jesus?
No turning back, no turning back.
—Author: (attributed to) S. Sundar Singh

Despite what has come and come what may, no turning back, friend, no turning back.

When the pain of your loss leaves you breathless, remember the One who gives breath to your lungs. When you don't even have the strength to stand, look to Him, and He will meet you where you are and as you are with open arms as your loving Father.

In the darkest places of your soul, in your deepest pain, and in the midst of your greatest loss, hope can be found in Jesus because He *is* hope. As you have lain weeping, reading the pages of this book, I hope you have found that to be true. And as you walk each day forward choosing to trust Jesus, I know for certain that you will.

Father, I believe You have seen all my pain. I believe You hold all the tears I've cried. I believe all three babies I have lost are safe with You. I believe You work all things for good. I believe You are working in my life. I believe You have compassion on me and my weakness and frailty. I believe that You love me and that I am Your daughter. I believe that everything I have is from You and through You. I believe that You know my heart's desire to have a family—that You made me this way. I believe that You have plans and purposes for my life and for these losses. I believe that You are good and faithful even when nothing makes sense. I believe that You are always worthy of praise and honor. I believe that this world is not my home and that through Jesus, You have saved me and have prepared an eternal heavenly home for me. I believe that You're actively involved in every second of every day in my life. Father, I believe in You, and I'll never turn back. Amen.

Printed in the United States
by Baker & Taylor Publisher Services